GLORIOUS INTERIORS

GLORIOUS INTERIORS

Needlepoint, knitting and decorative design projects for your home

KAFFE FASSETT

LITTLE BROWN AND COMPANY
Boston • New York • Toronto • London

This book is dedicated to all those with a touch of gypsy who share my vision.

First published in the United Kingdom in 1995 by Ebury Press Limited
Random House, 20 Vauxhall Bridge Road, London SW1V 2SA

First American Edition

ISBN 0-316-27506-9

Library of Congress Catalog Card Number 95-76260

10 9 8 7 6 5 4 3 2 1

Published simultaneously in Canada by Little Brown & Company (Canada) Limited

Editor: Sally Harding
Art Director: Polly Dawes
Photographer: Debbie Patterson
Copy Editor: Mary Remnant
Needlepoint Charts: Colin Salmon
Technical Illustrations: Sally Holmes
Knitting Charts and Rag Rug Diagrams: R & B Creative Services Ltd

Printed in Italy

contents

introduction

The only room decoration I can remember in the log cabin I grew up in on the coast of California was colourful cushions and a few paintings dotted about the timber walls. My mother did love collecting exotic oriental objects though. One cabinet was reserved entirely for Chinese bowls; and she would bring out an ancient Indian mirror cloth to cover the bucket under our Christmas tree. She also encouraged us kids to beat gold tin-can-top ornaments with a ball-peen hammer so they would shimmer on the tree. It was always my job to make papier-mâché angels and hand paint all the Christmas cards.

My parents' dream was to create a relaxed country restaurant and they had a Frank Lloyd Wright student design one, joined to our log house. Even though my mother came from a so-called 'good family' we were classed as Bohemian, largely because of my parents building and running 'that colourful restaurant' in Big Sur. Outside our circle was, I knew, a world where people had their houses 'done'. I was very dismissive of grand, expensive interiors because of the underlying feeling of nervousness lest one should make a mark on the new wallpaper, spill tea on the antique carpet, or break a rare porcelain. There was, I recall, a sterile beigeness to the most expensive of these places that chilled me to the core.

My grandmother had a very grand ranch house gorgeously furnished with oriental carpets, old Italian pots and wonderful embroideries; but that 'don't breathe or you might upset something' atmosphere kept me from ever enjoying it as a child. Later, her husband 'threw her out' as she put it, and my grandmother was reduced to a small cottage in Carmel, California, into which she crammed what treasures she had escaped with. Nice marquetry furniture, some good rugs and embroideries, and all the old books in her many bookcases arranged by colour groups. This cosier atmosphere was more to my liking.

My own sense of fantasy and fun in interiors developed later from seeing artists' houses and old paintings of exotic rooms. An artist who helped start my parents' restaurant and designed our phoenix-bird logo was Zev Harris. His style and confidence was a strong early influence. He had moved to an unfashionable part of California and built Crazy Crescent, a fantasy of a house. The bathroom had a wall constructed entirely of coloured bottles. Mosaics and pieces of wood decorated every surface of the house that wasn't covered with his whimsical paintings.

After art school, on my visits to Europe, I loved seeing lashings of colour and pattern in elegant room settings. Many great British houses made wonderful use of porcelains, carpets and patterned floors – an exciting mix of oriental and European antiques.

From Britain I travelled to Scandinavia with its painted furniture and handspun weaving, then on to Holland where porcelain and tiles were so wonderfully used, and tapestries brought a theatrical dimension to rooms. France and Italy were full of radiant marble, sumptuous brocades, and luxuriant wall and ceiling murals. But Morocco, where even primitive little tea houses would sport sky blue walls and vivid turquoise chairs, had perhaps the most fanciful interiors. The arrangements of small vases of flowers and dishes of fruit in these rooms transported one into an oriental painting!

One Moroccan room I particularly recall was in a little villa decorated all over the outside with pebbles worked in curly designs. The inside was delightfully smothered in flowery jugs, bright carpets and tile murals. The ceiling was covered with a swirling pattern in bold white and burgundy. It was as if

ABOVE: The mood setter for my dining room with a leaf theme (pages 110 and 111) was wallpaper from Alexander Beauchamp.

someone had given a pot of money to a gypsy child, and said, you can furnish this place with whatever your heart desires. The grand people who visited this interior with me were aghast, not least because I so enjoyed the playful exuberance of it all!

The closest I have come in my past work to interior decorating was to paint murals. In the seventies and eighties I did several large landscape murals. They often had the quality of old tapestries with borders of birds, leaves, cabbages, etc. The change of atmosphere these floor to ceiling works produced in the space they occupied was remarkable. They created a window into another world.

Even the smaller-scale murals I did, like the Persian miniature trees painted in a hallway in Hampstead, imbued the atmosphere with a special sense of space. I always overloaded these murals with sumptuous detail. This sumptuousness was especially evident in a sunset landscape painted in a laquer-red room in London. After I had spent months on an intense border of flowers, vegetables and birds, the commissioner of said mural painted over it the day after completion! It now waits there under three layers of paint and varnish to be unearthed.

One of my most successful murals was in a blue and white bathroom in a large house in the West Country in England. The client had an old Portuguese tile panel over the bathtub and wanted a similar baroque treatment on the three remaining walls and the floor. I broke all these surfaces into squares to make them look like they were covered with tiles. Then I painted motifs that echoed the original tiles on to the squares.

ABOVE: My fated red dining room mural. TOP: My Hampstead hallway mural. LEFT: Watts Towers (see page 84) was early proof for me that magic exists!

My most recent interiors commission was for two very large needlepoint tapestries for a Norwegian cruise liner; they were needed as a focal point for a public lounge. Since the floor, walls and furniture were a mixture of smoky blue and rather neutral tones, I stitched a seascape in faded colours bordered by large shells.

After many years of designing cushions, carpets, garments and wall hangings, I longed to create the encompassing surroundings that would really bring them to life. The notion that I could co-ordinate wall and floor coverings, fireplace and window treatments – particularly for schemes I wouldn't necessarily live in but would love to experience for a visit – was a thrill. I had recently purchased the ground floor in my house so was able to turn the extra rooms into one set after another. Although most of my sets went on to become other sets which were in the end converted back to more functional spaces, the one interior that I couldn't bare to disband was the leaf dining room. I have kept it and continue to enjoy its lush wallpaper mural and tapestry covered table.

When designing my interiors, I usually started with one decorative object. This object was always one that had an ornamental surface so captivating that it was a natural inspiration for further variations. Its theme and colourings were strong enough to serve as a mood setter and a common thread for an entire interior space.

ABOVE: Working from a panel of Portuguese tiles, I painted this West Country bathroom to look tiled throughout.

Once I had determined the central theme in this way, I could explore subtle variations – playing with scale, colour and tones simultaneously. Each new patterned surface that I added to the growing interiors seemed to effortlessly spark off the next until my room was a delightfully encrusted party cake.

All my early influences led me to my key approach to the interiors I design – that a room should reveal the occupier's sense of witty enjoyment, as well as their sense of beauty and taste. My room sets reveal a search for compatible objects whether antique or junk-shop finds that enhance the hand-made furnishings. I can think of no greater pleasure than rooting about in a flea market or junk stall looking for a collection of objects that expand each other's qualities.

You will begin to sense that I love rooms where as many surfaces as possible are crawling with pattern. The oriental pattern-on-pattern effects have always excited me. These teaming surfaces are sometimes faded and weathered until fabrics and wallpapers blend into a mysterious harmony, but remain disparate worlds of pattern dancing together all the same.

Heavily patterned surfaces are also the domain of Slavic peasants who paint every inch of their possessions with flowers, leaves and curlicues, then pose before them dripping in embroidered and beaded skirts, jackets, aprons and head-dresses. I also love old junk shops with dusty shelves of bric-à-brac crammed with the unexpected, and shambolic houses of eccentrics that look the same. Personal museums that are far too full of obsessive collections also celebrate the patterned surface. One such place, Snowshill Manor in the English Cotswolds, tickles me to the core. This Jacobean house is chock-a-block with Japanese armour, antique farm tools and bicycles, musical instruments, and boxes of beetles and butterflies.

Another colourful influence for me is the world of fairgrounds and circuses – vulgar colour and pattern with a liberal dash of glitz. Set to infectious music, the merry-go-rounds undulating with horses and flashing with mirrors never fail to bring out the childish wonder in me. I see that same exciting sense of saturated design on the Indian, Pakistani and Afghani trucks whose every possible

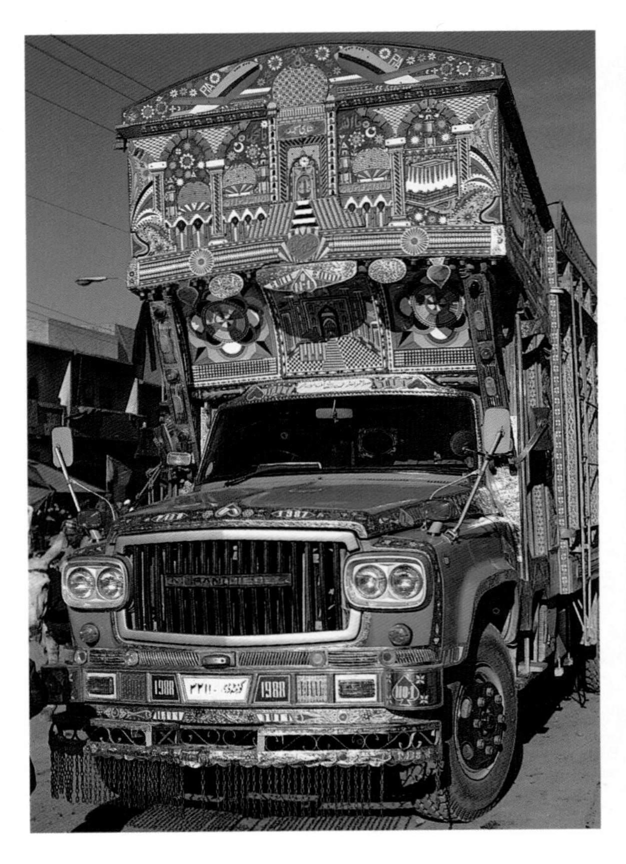

ABOVE: A Pakistani truck transformed by all-over geometry and colour. Bravo! ABOVE RIGHT: A Hungarian girl from Transylvania shining in an ornately embroidered peasant dress.

surface is vibrating with colour and shapes. They transform the pedestrian into a magical vision that makes our spirits soar.

On my first trip to an Afghani desert town I had collapsed in a heap on a porch waiting for the midday heat to subside. There was little to drink and my head was weighed down with near delirium. Suddenly, a huge truck painted all over with a jet plane surrounded by roses and fancy scrolls came barrelling down the road like an apparition. My thirst vanished the instant I beheld this delectable flight of fancy.

My desire in this book is to create rooms that dance with pattern and vibrate with colourful texture. Looking for media that best perform this trick brought me to rag rugs, collage and mosaic. Collage and mosaic are the arts of making new patterns from fragments of old ones. Rag rugs too create lively surfaces from the texture of shredded printed cloth and old clothes.

If some or all of this book is too busy and too strong in colour for you, take the textures and apply them to as subtle a palette as suits your day-to-day life. Rag rugs done in the grey shades of stones or in soft beiges would be elegant. Collages can be composed of whites and off whites, like a mosaic mirror frame I've just made of white crockery. Needlepoint and knitting can be done in very muted tones which might be more peaceful to live with.

At the moment, I am creating a room for myself that is mostly white, off white, ochre and soft beige tones. 'Amazing!' I hear my friends cry who have lived through my over-the-top rooms. But I do hope to find many different textures and many shades of white to create a subtle complexity that reveals itself slowly, always important in any work of art. To me, a well designed room is an artistic expression and should be a continuing joy to live in.

squares

Because squares form so neatly into grids, they are the most straightforward of the building blocks of design. A simple chequerboard is a timeless classic layout for floors, bedcovers and wall hangings. Old paving stones in a thousand tones of blue-greys, pinky-greys, browns and ochres roughly cut into square shapes astound me with their beauty every time I set eyes on them.

Inspired by designs such as these I have returned to a squares format again and again in my work.

The squares designs in this chapter have been kept fairly simple, but squares can get wildly intricate if you start to play with them. The amazing fractals on computers appear to me as millions of square designs endlessly rearranging themselves – very similar to the inside of my head at times!

The Boston painter Peter Plamondon's painted stack of Chinese takeaway boxes (page 16) is a unique study of squares. A good example of squares that many will have been struck by on their travels is the hill villages of Turkey and Greece – square houses dotted with square windows and rectangular doors, overlapping up a hillside.

Though they can work effectively as an all-over design in their own right, squares also act as wonderfully exuberant backgrounds for flowers, fans, circles

LEFT: The idea of a postage-stamp lampshade occurred to me after seeing walls covered with stamps in a Caribbean room.
OVERLEAF: The squares bedroom started with the antique postage-stamp quilt hanging on the wall.

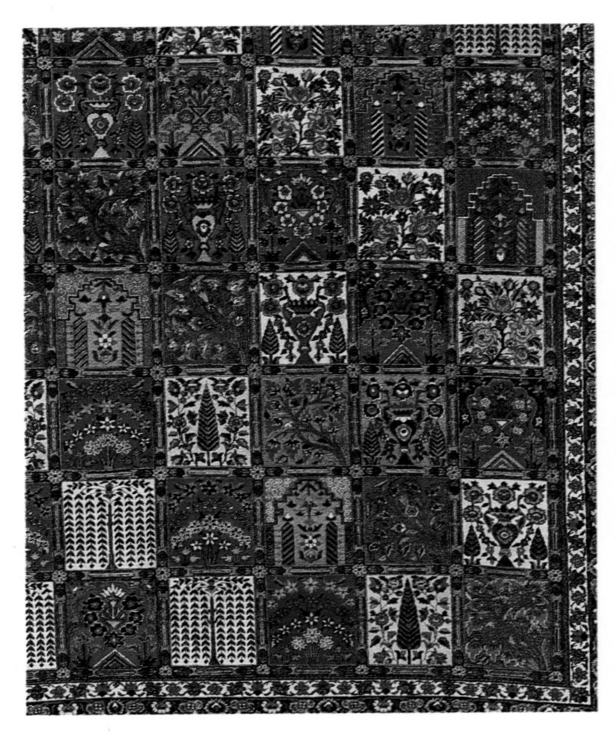

ABOVE: Boston artist Peter Plamondon's painting of boxes. TOP RIGHT: Shell grotto at Leeds Castle in Kent with square motifs. TOP LEFT: Baktiari carpet displaying an intricate treatment of the squares theme. LEFT: Village kitchen with my collection of square tiles amassed over a period of years. RIGHT: *Decorated Boxes* and *Overlapping Squares Cushions*.

or any manner of motif. Any book on old patchwork quilts will show you instantly how many variations have been conjured up with simple squares. Art deco decoration is another excellent source of angular ideas.

The mood-setter and springboard for my room design based on squares is a quilt dating back to the late 1800s. A supreme example of the straightforward chequerboard pattern in all its glory, this postage-stamp quilt has fascinated everyone who has seen it. How could such a vast field of minute fingernail - sized scraps of material have been so painstakingly and beautifully put together? With love and passion, say I! I salute its maker, for despite the amazingly large variety of pattern and colour, the minute square patches still merge together to form a strong and compelling overall design.

Far from dismissing this most elementary of structures, I still embrace the square as a central design element over and over in my new work. Once I found the postage-stamp quilt, I was delighted to use it as the common denominator for a whole roomful of dancing squares.

The first thing I observed about the colour of the postage-stamp quilt was the absence of any clean white. It is a symphony of many soft creams and combinations of red and

cream, blue and cream, and black and cream. Other important recurring colours are sage green and a golden yellow, which help create the diamond shapes in the arrangement. The reds are never too clean or harsh, but are deep husky vermilions. Flickers of orange occur to liven up the quilt, sparking up the pink and yellow.

To create a dappled surface for the bedroom interior I covered the walls with a collage of paper patches cut from several rolls of flowered wallpaper. Because the postage-stamp quilt is constructed in diagonal stripes of its various patterns I used the same format for my collaged walls. The sage green, pink, blue and cream of the quilt influenced my choices of wallpapers. I didn't want anything too sharp or too mushy, but instead chose papers with an antique print look that had harmonious but alive colours.

By sorting the 3½-inch squares of wallpaper into piles of lighter and darker tones, I was able to create enough contrast in my diagonal stripes. It is fascinating how different parts of this large repeat pattern appear so varied, yet the overall effect is harmonized by the framework of striped rows. Expanding the variation in my wallpaper even further, I occasionally inserted a different floral patterned square in a diagonal stripe to give the collage a tile-like appearance. I have observed this refreshing visual effect in Moroccan tiled walls where one or two tiles in the repeat pattern are quite different or made up of odd broken tiles.

After deciding on the wall covering for my squares room, I went on to design the knitted and crocheted *Fiesta Squares Afghan*. The larger blocks of squares on the afghan create a lively contrast with the tiny scale of the quilt's design. Each of the square patches of the afghan is knitted in a chequerboard pattern of softly contrasting shades. The joined patches are edged with a diagonal striped crochet border and a final row of crocheted scallops.

After the predictable chequerboard patterns on the walls and the afghan, it was fun to break into the playful colour changes in the knitted *Decorated Boxes Cushion* (page 25) and the variegated striped boxes in the *Celebration Squares Rag Rug* (page 26). The knitted cushion design reminds me of mosaic designs on Venetian floors. It is also the perfect simple format for your own original colour combinations.

Fiesta Squares Afghan

Size of afghan

The finished afghan measures 141cm (55½in) square. Each square patch measures approximately 23.5cm (9¼in) square.

Materials

• PATERNA/YAN *Persian Yarn* in the following 19 colours:

Light sky blue	585	243m (265yd)
Dark federal blue	501	211m (231yd)
Medium sky blue	583	75m (82yd)
Donkey brown	473	155m (170yd)
Dark dusty pink	911	80m (87yd)
Light fawn brown	405	416m (455yd)
Autumn yellow	724	69m (75yd)
Dark pearl grey	211	307m (336yd)
Strawberry	951	64m (70yd)
Pale golden brown	445	180m (196yd)
Light salmon	845	149m (162yd)
Medium forest green	603	85m (93yd)

1	2	3	4	5	6
7	8	9	10	11	12
13	14	15	16	17	18
19	20	21	22	23	24
25	26	27	28	29	30
31	32	33	34	35	36

ABOVE: This diagram shows the positions for the completed patches on the *Fiesta Squares Afghan*.

Hot pink	963	95m (104yd)
Light pine green	664	228m (249yd)
Cream	263	138m (151yd)
Light pearl grey	212	171m (187yd)
Fuchsia	354	30m (33yd)
Beige brown	463	111m (122yd)
Rusty rose	933	19m (20yd)

- One pair of 5mm (US size 8) knitting needles
- 5mm (US size H) crochet hook
- Blunt-ended yarn needle for joining patches

Knitting stitch gauge

18 sts and 19 rows to 10cm (4in) measured over Fair Isle check pattern using all three strands of the Persian Yarn and 5mm (US size 8) knitting needles. Each knitted square measures approximately 13cm (5 ¼in) square after blocking.

Special notes

The afghan is made up of 36 square patches. The centre of each patch is knitted and the border and scalloped edging are crocheted. Each of the squares is made in exactly the same way but in a different colourway (see *Colourway table* on following page).
All three strands of the Persian Yarn are used together throughout. See page 157 for calculating number of skeins or hanks required. When purchasing Persian Yarn for knitting, be sure to purchase continuous skeins/hanks instead of lengths already precut for needlepoint.

Knitted square no. 1

Following the *Colourway table* for the colours for square no. 1, cast on 24 sts using knitting needles and yarn A.
Work the check pattern using the Fair Isle method, stranding the colour not in use across the wrong side of the knitting and weaving it around the working yarn so that there are no loose ends at back of work.
(See page 157 for knitting abbreviations.)
Using yarns A and B (see *Colourway table),* begin bicolour check pattern as follows:
1st row (WS) [With A p4, with B p4] 3 times.
2nd row [With B k4, with A k4] 3 times.

ABOVE: The basic chequerboard pattern on the square patches makes the *Fiesta Squares Afghan* the simplest of knits.

3rd–5th rows Rep first and 2nd rows once more, then rep first row once, so ending with a p row.
6th row (RS) [With A k4, with B k4] 3 times.
7th row [With B p4, with A p4] 3 times.
8th–10th rows Rep 6th and 7th rows once more, then rep 6th row once, so ending with a k row.
Rep first–10th rows once more, then rep first–5th rows once, so ending with a p row. (Total of 25 rows worked.)
Break off yarn A.
Cast (bind) off with yarn B.
Press the finished knitted square on the WS with a damp cloth and a warm iron.
Before beginning the next knitted square, complete the patch by working the crochet border.

Crochet border

The crochet border is worked in a total of 7 rounds. The first 5 rounds are worked in double crochet (US single crochet) and the last 2 rounds form the scalloped edging. The scalloped edging is formed by working double crochet (US single crochet) and half treble crochet (US half double crochet) on a base round of chain-stitch loops. Note that the instructions are written using the UK terms for the crochet stitches, with the US terms in parentheses (turn to page 157 for a full explanation of UK and US crochet terminology).
Using crochet hook and working in rounds with the RS always facing, begin the crochet border as follows:
1st rnd Using C (see *Colourway table* for colours), join yarn with a slip st between the 2nd and 3rd st at the top right-hand corner of knitted square no. 1, work 1ch, 1dc(sc) into same place that slip st was worked, work 17dc(sc) more evenly along top of square, then work 3dc(sc) into corner, *work 18dc(sc) evenly along next side of square, work 3dc(sc) in next corner,* rep from * to * twice more, then using yarn D join with a slip st to first dc(sc) of rnd. Do not turn at end of rounds. (84 sts)

Colourway table

	Knitted square		Crochet stripes			Crochet checks		Scallops
Patch	A	B	C	D	E	F	G	H
1	501	585	951	211	263	405	211	473
2	583	473	933	212	263	405	211	664
3	911	405	933	501	445	405	211	212
4	724	211	963	212	263	845	501	585
5	585	951	963	603	263	405	501	473
6	445	473	354	211	263	845	211	664
7	845	911	354	211	445	405	501	664
8	603	445	724	463	263	405	501	405
9	603	963	911	212	263	405	473	585
10	583	585	911	211	445	405	501	664
11	911	845	963	212	263	405	211	585
12	845	603	951	583	445	405	211	463
13	445	473	845	211	263	405	501	405
14	664	951	963	212	263	405	501	664
15	911	664	951	501	263	405	501	212
16	603	263	963	583	445	405	501	463
17	212	724	933	212	263	405	501	405
18	501	724	845	211	445	405	211	664
19	473	583	354	501	445	405	211	211
20	664	445	951	211	445	405	211	585
21	354	211	845	212	445	405	211	463
22	724	585	963	212	263	405	501	664
23	585	911	963	211	263	405	501	212
24	405	664	583	211	845	405	211	585
25	212	845	963	212	263	405	211	473
26	463	585	963	211	445	845	501	664
27	911	212	845	211	445	405	501	585
28	583	963	724	501	445	405	501	212
29	585	263	845	211	445	405	211	664
30	845	463	963	211	445	405	501	211
31	845	583	951	211	445	405	211	463
32	585	603	845	501	445	405	211	585
33	263	724	963	463	445	405	211	473
34	603	445	845	473	445	405	501	405
35	603	501	845	211	445	405	211	585
36	664	951	963	212	263	405	211	473

Break off yarn C.
2nd rnd Using D, work 1ch, 1dc(sc) into same place that slip st was worked, 1dc(sc) into each of next 18dc(sc), 3dc(sc) into next dc(sc) which is centre st of 3dc(sc)-group, *1dc(sc) into each of next 20dc(sc), 3dc(sc) into next dc(sc),* rep from * to * twice more, 1dc(sc) into last dc(sc), then using yarn E join with a slip st to first dc(sc) of rnd. (92 sts)

Break off yarn D.

3rd rnd Using E, work 1ch, 1dc(sc) into same dc(sc) that slip st was worked, 1dc(sc) into each of next 19dc(sc), 3dc(sc) into next dc(sc) which is centre st of 3dc(sc)-group, ⋆1dc(sc) into each of next 22dc(sc), 3dc(sc) into next dc(sc),⋆ rep from ⋆ to ⋆ twice more, 1dc(sc) into each of last 2dc(sc), then using yarn F join with a slip st to first dc(sc) of rnd. (100 sts)

Break off yarn E.

Working over the yarn not in use, work bicolour checks with yarns F and G on next 2 rnds as follows:

4th rnd With F work 1ch, 1dc(sc) into same dc(sc) that slip st was worked, 1dc(sc) into each of next 2dc(sc), ⋆with G 1dc(sc) into each of next 3dc(sc), with F 1dc(sc) into each of next 3dc(sc),⋆ rep from ⋆ to ⋆ twice more, ⋆⋆with G 3dc(sc) into next dc(sc), with F 1dc(sc) into each of next 3dc(sc), rep from ⋆ to ⋆ 3 times, with G 3dc (sc) into each of next 3dc(sc), with F 3dc(sc) into next (corner) dc(sc),⋆⋆ rep from ⋆ to ⋆ 4 times, rep from ⋆⋆ to ⋆⋆ once, with G work 1dc(sc) into each of last 3dc(sc) of rnd, then still using yarn G join with a slip st to first dc(sc). (108 sts)

5th rnd With G work 1ch, 1dc(sc) into same dc(sc) that slip st was worked, ⋆with F 1dc(sc) into each of next 3dc(sc), with G 1dc(sc) into each of next 3dc(sc),⋆ rep from ⋆ to ⋆ twice more, ⋆⋆with F 1dc(sc) into each of next 3dc(sc), with G 2dc(sc) into next dc(sc) which is corner st, with G 1dc(sc) into each of next 2dc(sc), rep from ⋆ to ⋆ 4 times, with F 2dc(sc) into next dc(sc), with F 1dc(sc) into each of next 2dc(sc),⋆⋆ with G 1dc(sc) into each of next 3dc(sc), rep from ⋆ to ⋆ 3 times, rep from ⋆⋆ to ⋆⋆ once, with G 1dc(sc) into each of last 2dc(sc), then still using G join with a slip st to first dc(sc). (112 sts)

With F work 1 slip st into top of each of next 2dc(sc), then with H work 1 slip st into next dc(sc) to reach position of beginning of next rnd.

Break off yarns F and G.

Using yarn H only, work the scalloped edging over next 2 rnds as follows:

6th rnd ⋆Work 4ch, skip next 3dc(sc) and work 1 slip st into next dc(sc),⋆ rep from ⋆ to ⋆ 26 times more, work 4ch, then join with a slip st to first slip st of rnd. (28 four-ch loops)

7th rnd ⋆[Work 2dc(sc), 3htr(hdc), 2dc(sc)] all into next 4-ch loop,⋆ rep from ⋆ to ⋆ to end of rnd, then join with a slip st to first slip st of rnd. Fasten off.

This completes first afghan patch. Write number '1' on a piece of scrap paper and pin it to the finished patch.

Make remaining 35 patches in same way, following the *Colourway table* for the colours for each patch and labeling each patch after completion.

Joining the afghan patches

Using yarn needle and one of the scalloped edging colours, join patch nos. 1–6 first (see page 18). Join the patches with oversewing (overcasting) stitches between the htr(hdc) of each of the adjacent scallops, running the needle through the crochet stitches between each join.

After joining the first row of patches in this way, join patch no. 7 to patch no. 1, then join patch no. 8 to patch no. 7 and patch no. 2.

Continue in this way along the second row of patches, then join each of the remaining rows of patches in the same way.

Outer scalloped edging

After all the patches have been joined, work a scalloped edging around the outer edge of the afghan as follows:

1st rnd (RS) Using Paterna Persian Yarn shade no. 405 and with RS facing, join yarn with a slip st to any centre htr(hdc) of a scallop on the outer edge of the afghan, ⋆work 4ch, work 1 slip st into centre htr(hdc) of the next scallop,⋆ rep from ⋆ to ⋆ all around outer edge to last scallop, work 4ch, then join with a slip st to first slip st of rnd.

2nd rnd Work as for 7th rnd of crochet border. Fasten off.

Overlapping Squares Cushion

Size of cushion

The finished cushion measures 40cm (16in) wide by 41cm (16 1/4in) tall.

Materials

- 10-mesh single- or double-thread canvas 56cm (22in) square
- APPLETON wool tapestry yarn in the 12 colours listed below
- Size 18 tapestry needle
- 70cm (3/4yd) of 90cm (36in) wide backing fabric and matching sewing thread
- 1.8m (2yd) of piping (filling) cord or ready-made cord (optional)
- 33cm (13in) zipper
- Cushion pad (pillow form) same size as finished cover or slightly larger

Yarn colours and amounts

You will need Appleton wool tapestry yarn (10m/11yd skeins) in the following 12 colours and approximate amounts:

A	Dark royal blue	826	2 skeins
B	Light turquoise	522	4 skeins
C	Purple	104	4 skeins
D	Dark terracotta	126	3 skeins
E	Autumn yellow	475	5 skeins
F	Pale coral	861	4 skeins
G	Mid rose pink	944	4 skeins
H	Light rose pink	942	3 skeins
I	Pale rose pink	751	3 skeins
J	Orange red	447	4 skeins
K	Early English green	544	4 skeins
L	Bright lime	997	3 skeins

Working the embroidery

The chart is 162 stitches wide and 164 stitches tall. Begin by marking the outline of the design on to your canvas and, if desired, dividing it into tens just like the charted design. Make a paper template of the design outline and set aside to use later as a guide for blocking.

Following the chart on right, work the embroidery in tent stitch, using one strand

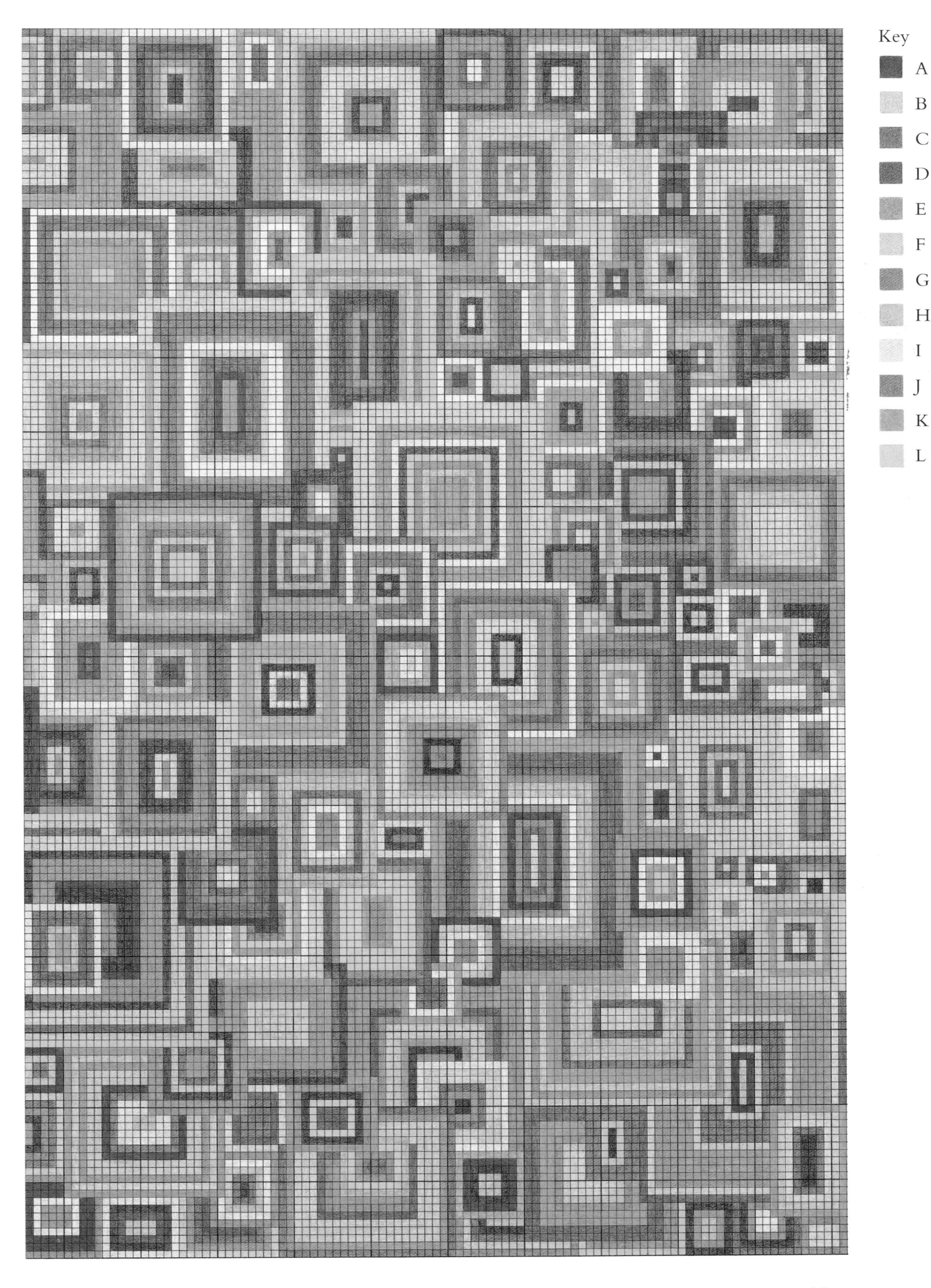
Key
A
B
C
D
E
F
G
H
I
J
K
L

of Appleton wool tapestry yarn (see page 150 for tent stitch techniques).

Finishing the cushion cover

After the embroidery has been completed, block the canvas, using the paper template as your guide (see page 152).

Trim the canvas edges, leaving a seam allowance of 2cm (3/4in).

Sew the zipper between two pieces of fabric for the cushion cover back as instructed on page 152.

If desired, cover the piping (filling) cord and pin to the needlepoint. Then join the front and back of the cover as described on page 152. If you are using a ready-made cord as a trimming, sew it to the completed cover, tucking the ends into a small opening in the seam.

Decorated Boxes Cushion

Size of cushion

The finished cushion measures 48cm (19¼in) wide by 46cm (18¼in) tall.

Materials

- Rowan *Lightweight DK* (25g/1oz hanks) in the following 14 colours:

A	Dark steel blue	52	1 hank
B	Rust	26	2 hanks
C	Pale pink	68	2 hanks
D	Light blue	123	1 hank
E	Mauve	96	1 hank
F	Mustard	8	1 hank
G	Bright gold	14	1 hank
H	Royal blue	57	2 hanks
J	Rose pink	66	1 hank
L	Green	605	2 hanks
M	Cream	4	1 hank
N	Medium blue	50	1 hank
O	Dusty rose	69	1 hank
Q	Orange	23	1 hank

- One pair of 3¾mm (US size 5) knitting needles
- Small piece of scrap fabric for backing the knitting
- 70cm (¾yd) of 90cm (36in) wide fabric

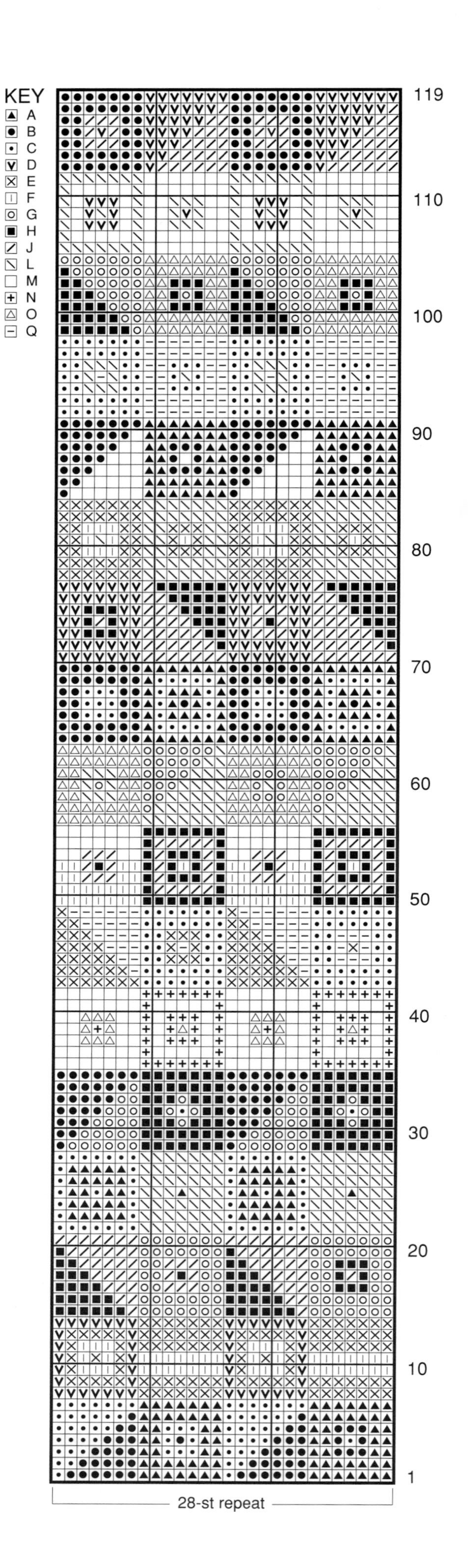

for cushion cover back and matching sewing thread
- 43cm (17in) zipper
- Cushion pad (pillow form) same size as finished cover or slightly larger

Knitting stitch gauge

26 sts and 26 rows to 10cm (4in) measured over colourwork pattern using $3^3/_4$mm (US size 5) knitting needles.

Special notes

When working the colourwork pattern, use the Fair Isle technique. There are two or three colours used in each row. Carry the colour not in use loosely across the WS of the square, weaving it in every 3 or 4 sts to avoid long loose ends.

Read chart from right to left for k (RS odd-numbered) rows and from left to right for p (WS even-numbered) rows.

Charted decorated boxes design

Using yarn A, cast on 126 sts.
Beg with a k row, work 119 rows in st st following chart for colourwork pattern (see special notes) and working 28-st repeat 4 times across each row, ending each k row with first 14 sts of chart and beginning each p row with same 14 sts but worked from left to right.
Using yarn B, cast (bind) off.

Finishing the cushion cover

Press lightly on WS with a damp cloth and a warm iron.
Cut a piece of scrap fabric the same size as the knitting plus a 1.5cm ($^1/_2$in) seam allowance all around the edge.
With the wrong sides facing each other, pin the knitting to the centre of this piece of fabric. Then sew the two layers together, working small running stitches very close to the edge of the knitting.
Sew the zipper between two pieces of fabric for the cushion cover back and join the front and back of the cover as instructed on page 152, catching the edge of the knitting into the seam.

ABOVE: The *Decorated Boxes Cushion* could be done in any group of colours to match your room.

Celebration Squares Rag Rug

Size of rag rug

The finished rag rug measures 75cm (30in) wide by 125cm (50in) long.

Materials

- Piece of loose-weave hessian (burlap) at least 91cm (36in) by 141cm (56in)
- Variety of scrap fabrics for strips (see *Choosing the colours* below)
- Large rug hook
- 4.3m ($4^3/_4$yd) of 6cm ($2^1/_2$in) wide twilled carpet binding tape (optional)
- Strong thread for hemming

Choosing the colours

You will need scrap fabrics in a variety of colours and in a range of tones. Study the photograph of the rug for an idea of the types of colours to choose. Then look for scraps to fit into this scheme or to fit into your own original palette. (See page 147 for

ABOVE: Once you have started this rag rug you'll find that the contrasting stripes of the squares practically hook themselves.

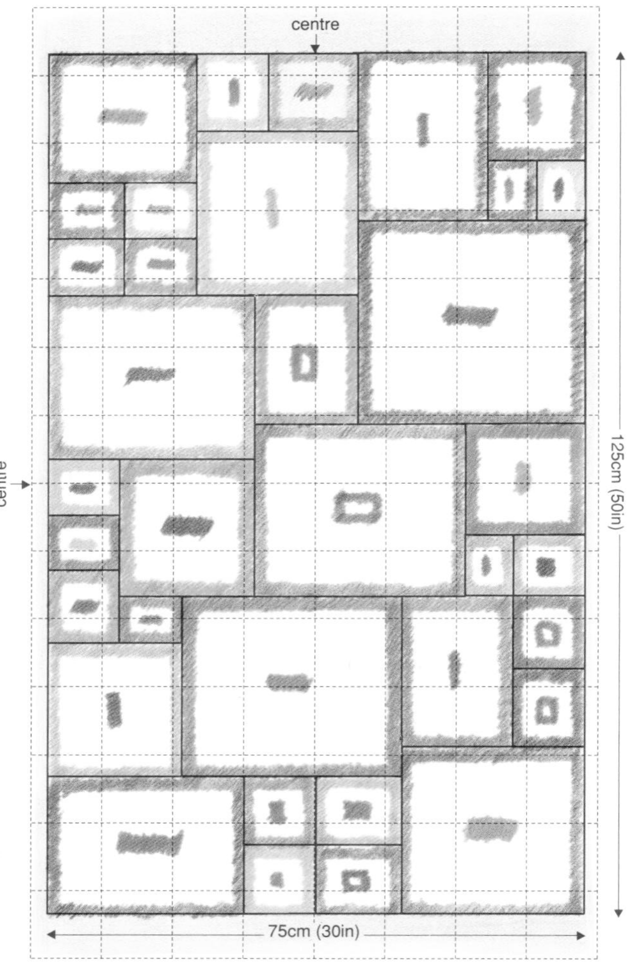

Note: Each square on the grid represents 10cm (4in).

detailed information on types of fabrics suitable for rag rugs.)

Transferring the design

Using a dressmaker's marking pen, mark the outer outline of the rug on to the right side of the hessian (burlap). The dimensions of the outer outline are given on the previous page, under *Size of rag rug,* and are shown on the rug design diagram. Allow at least 8cm (3in) of extra fabric all around the edge.

Transfer the rug design on to the right side of the fabric as instructed on page 148.

Preparing the rag strips

Cut some of the fabric scraps into strips 1.5cm (1/2in) to 2.5cm (1in) wide, depending on the thickness of the fabric. Cut only enough strips to provide a variety of tones and shades for working the first square. Cut the remaining scraps only when you need them as the work progresses.

A detailed explanation of how to cut strips for rag rugs is given on page 148.

Hooking the rug

Before starting to hook the rug, read the hooking instructions on page 149.

Then begin the rug by working the outer outline of one of the individual squares within the design, using a rag strip of the desired colour. (As a guideline, the rug diagram indicates the colour used for the outline of each separate square on the original *Celebration Squares Rag Rug.*) After completing this outline, choose a rag strip in a contrasting colour and work a second line of hooked loops just inside the first.

Continue in this way, working rows of concentric squares in stripes towards the centre of the square. After working each row of colour, check to see that it contrasts sufficiently with the previous row of colour.

When there is only room left for one or two more lines of loops within the square, finish with a contrasting centre.

Work each of the remaining squares in the same way. A very pleasing effect will be achieved if each individual square is given a different palette as on the original rug.

Finishing the rug

After the hooking has been completed, bind the edges of the hessian (burlap) if desired, then turn back the edges and work the hem, mitring the corners. Turn to page 149 for finishing instructions.

After the pastel haven of a bedroom I longed for something more full blooded and daring in the use of colour for a squares theme. My assistant Brandon was painting his country sitting room coral red and this lively colour scheme inspired me to begin the knitted *Red Squares Blanket.* I gathered together every shade of red and tweedy pink to hand, added colours that sparked or sang in that palette, and started to knit. Squares, even in very differing scales, are easy to improvise on the needle. After establishing a border for the blanket, I plunged into the large centre squares with enthusiasm. The result was so jolly that I had the blanket copied as a tufted carpet by the Edinburgh Tapestry Weavers (see right).

When finishing a large knitted blanket like this, I crochet two or three rows around it to help it lie flat. This also gives a chance to add a sharp bit of colour detail at the edge – usually in contrasting tones.

The *Square Patch Cushions* were composed by simply taking bright contrasting colours and doing the same variation of squares scale as on the blanket. I love the way the Indonesian fabric and the old kilim on the stairs in this coral room go with these modern knitting designs. It shows how much I'm influenced by ethnic patterns.

A wonderful example of an influence that has run through many of my overlapping patch designs is the patchwork of antique Indian embroideries behind the couch. The pieces in this large bedcover probably started life as the brilliant reds and magentas that India is so famous for. Now it has faded and mellowed to a mysteriously elegant montage. It is the sort of splendid example that inspires me to do patchworks of all my knitting stitch gauge swatches and colour trial squares. I once sold two panels of sample squares of knitting crocheted together to an Embassy as a decorative tapestry.

ABOVE: This bold tufted carpet design is based on my knitted throw featured on the following page.

Square Patch Cushion

Size of cushion

The finished knitted cushion measures 55cm (21½in) wide by 52cm (20¼in) tall including the striped border.

Materials

• ROWAN *Lightweight DK* (25g/1oz hanks) in the following 13 colours:

A	Red	44	2 hanks
B	Light green	416	2 hanks
C	Steel blue	52	1 hank
D	Coral	21	1 hank
E	Dark sea blue	54	1 hank
F	Grey	60	1 hank
G	Bright pink	19	1 hank
H	Cream	4	1 hank
J	Green	100	1 hank
L	Yellow	13	1 hank
M	Mauve	96	1 hank
N	Pale grey	120	1 hank
O	Orange	17	1 hank

• One pair each of 3¾mm (US size 5) and 4mm (US size 6) knitting needles
• Small piece of scrap fabric for backing the knitting
• 70cm (¾yd) of 90cm (36in) wide fabric for cushion cover back and matching sewing thread
• 48cm (19in) zipper
• Cushion pad (pillow form) same size as finished cover or slightly larger

Knitting stitch gauge

22 sts and 27 rows to 10cm (4in) measured over colourwork pattern using 4mm (US size 6) knitting needles.

Special notes

When working the colourwork pattern, use the intarsia method for working the individual square patches, using separate lengths of yarn for each striped square patch and linking one square patch to the next by twisting the yarns around each other on WS where they meet to avoid holes. Use the Fair Isle method for working each of the individual striped square patches, carrying the colour not in use loosely across the WS of the square and weaving it in every 3 or 4 sts to avoid long loose ends.
Read chart from right to left for k (RS odd-numbered) rows and from left to right for p (WS even-numbered) rows.

LEFT: The *Square Patch Cushions* sit handsomely in this setting with the rich red palette of the knitted throw.

Charted square patch design

Using smaller needles and yarn A, cast on 120 sts.
Beg with a p row, work 9 rows in st st, working first 3 rows in A, next 3 rows in B and last 3 rows in A, AND AT THE SAME TIME dec one st at each end of 3rd row and every foll row 6 times in all, then work one row without shaping, so ending with a p row. (108 sts)
Break off yarns A and B.
Change to larger needles and cont in st st throughout, work 124 rows, following chart for colourwork pattern (see special notes), so ending with a p row.
Change to smaller needles and work 9 rows in st st, working first 3 rows in A, next 3 rows in B and last 3 rows in A, AND AT THE SAME TIME dec inc one st at each end of 3rd row and every foll row 6 times in all, then work one row without shaping, so ending with a k row. (120 sts)
Using yarn A, cast (bind) off. Press lightly on WS with a damp cloth and a warm iron.

Striped side borders

With RS facing and using smaller needles and yarn A, pick up and knit 100 sts evenly along right-hand vertical edge of knitted piece between striped border at top and bottom. P one row.
K one row, inc one st at each end. (102 sts)
Change to yarn B and work 3 rows in st st, inc one st at each end of every row.
Break off yarn B.
Using yarn A and cont in st st, work 2 rows, inc one st at each end of both rows. (112 sts). Work one row without shaping.

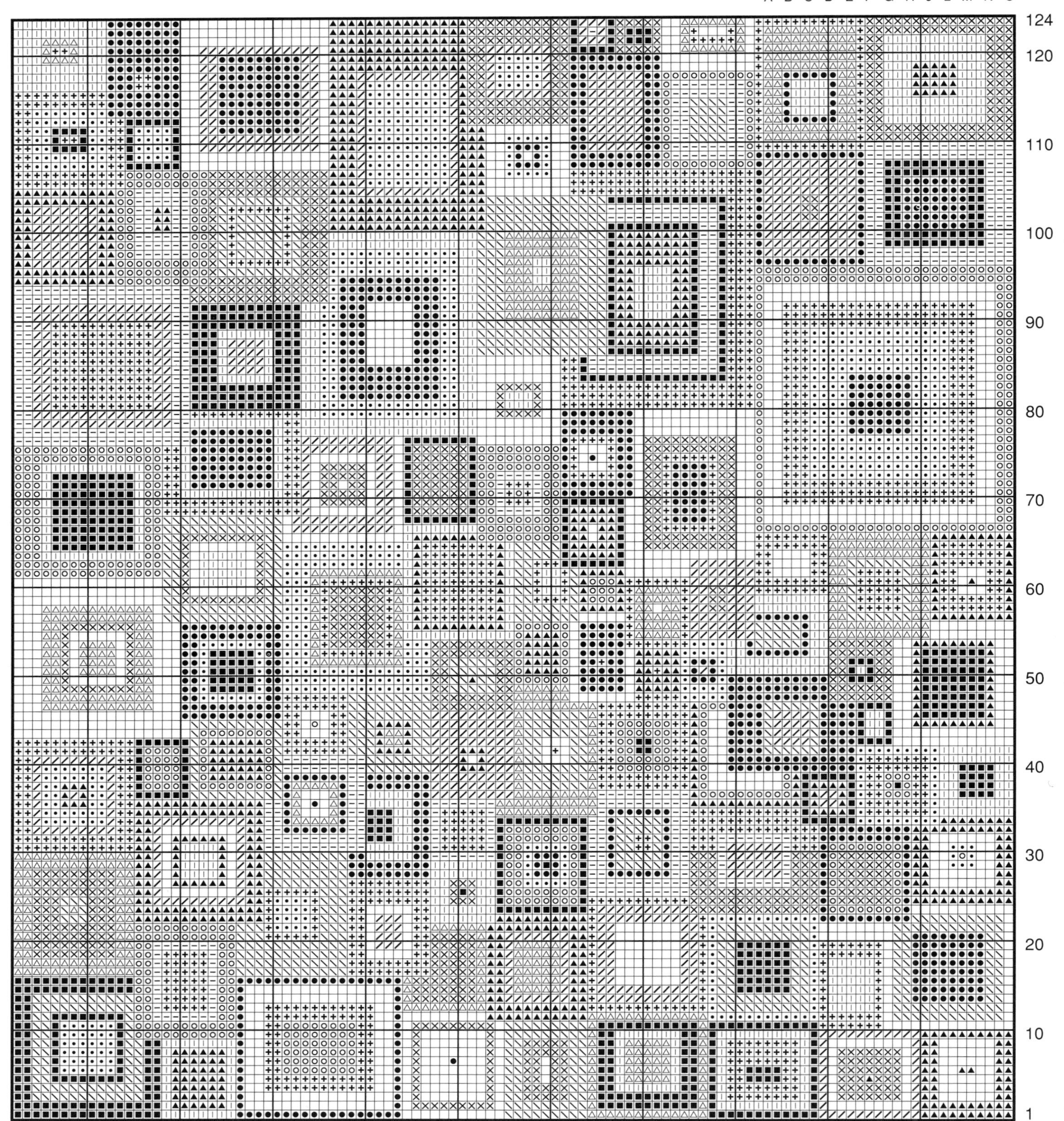

Still using yarns A, cast (bind) off.
Work border on rem edge in same way.

Finishing the cushion cover

Join mitred corner seams and press border.
Cut a piece of scrap fabric the same size as the knitting plus a 1.5cm (½in) seam allowance all around the edge.
With the wrong sides facing each other, pin the knitting to the centre of this piece of fabric. Then sew the two layers together, working small running stitches very close to the edge of the knitting.
Sew the zipper between two pieces of fabric for the cushion cover back and join the front and back of the cover as instructed on page 152, carefully catching the edge of the knitting into the seam.

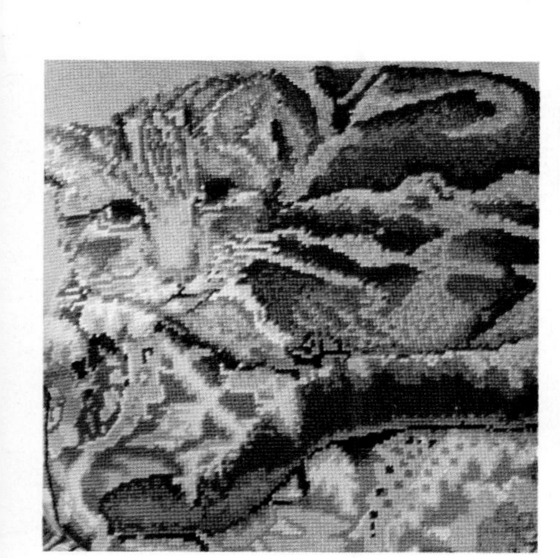

shells and animals

As I meander through great houses and museums of decorative arts, I notice that birds, animals and shells often feature as themes for furniture, tapestries, carved frames and architectural details. Shells cascade and drape in bowers to create borders; while birds form the subject of paintings, porcelains and tapestries.

Undoubtedly, the shell grotto displays one of the most joyous and outrageous patterned surfaces that has popped up through the centuries. The idea of walls and ceilings covered with these exquisite and flamboyant shapes plastered cheek by jowl is breathtaking. Geometric shell patterns with bordered panels of latticework are especially effective, as they seem to emphasize the architectural shapes of the grotto in a lively and handsome way.

Animals, particularly wild exotic ones, walk the jungles and forests of the great tapestries. The Orientals often created playful chairs and tables of carved monkeys. Peacocks became an obsession at the turn of the century, appearing on lamps, fabrics, fire screens, tiles, murals and stained glass.

LEFT: The golden tones of my marquetry boxes and wicker chair make a perfect backdrop for the *Shell Slippers*.
OVERLEAF: A restrained colour scheme makes the shells and animals room more of a texture story than most of my others.

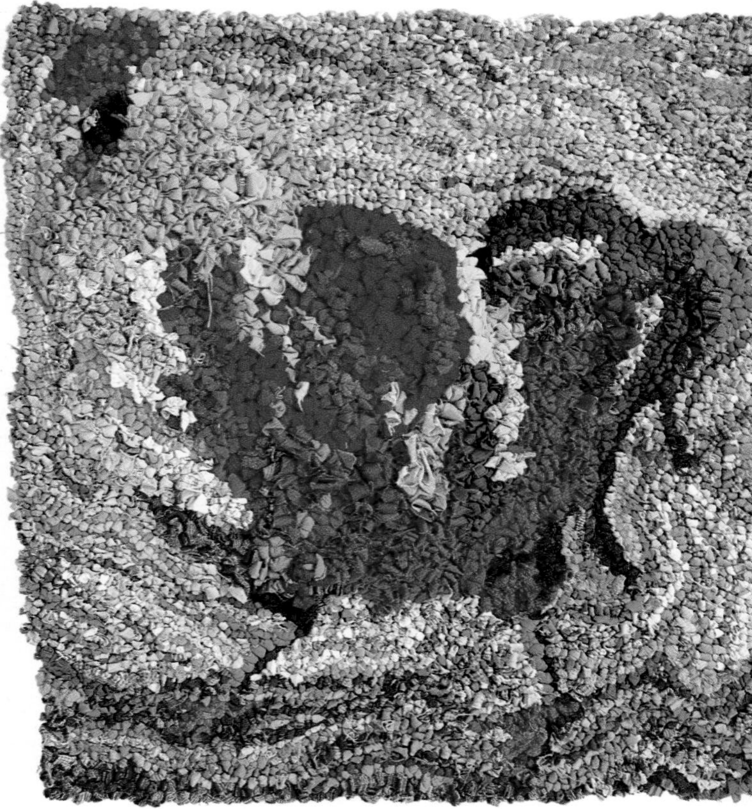

TOP: The sharp burnt oranges of the *Lobster* and *Crab Cushions* cut a dash in this scene of faded shell colours. ABOVE: Brandon Mably's spirited first attempt at rag rug hooking. LEFT: My *Shell Chair*.

ABOVE: The huge black areas on white of Friesian cows, in my opinion, has to be one of nature's boldest, most contrasting designs.

Exotic creatures of the wild have an undeniable beauty, but domestic farm animals captivate me with the nostalgic affection of childhood memories. Shells have also played a big part in my youth, spent living on the California coast and exploring rock pools at every opportunity.

Since shells and animals share a similar colour range, I combined them as a joint theme for a drawing room with a seaside feel. This interior treatment was built up around the neutral tones of my needlepoint *Shells on Sand Cushion*. The relative lack of bright hues called for soft putty-coloured walls to allow the neutral tones of this palette to shine.

I find the massing together of paintings or other objects in Victorian rooms intriguing. Encrusted with shell paintings and animal tapestries, this whole shells and animals drawing room has the feel of a Victorian shell-covered box. The way the shell-packed atmosphere spills on to the curtains, the shell needlepoint chair, and the crab and lobster cushions is just the effusive effect I was after.

There is something endlessly thrilling about the faded, washed-out tones and forms of shells. You will see from the wall in my shells and animals interior that I have often painted shells set alongside stones and old fabrics. A palette of chalky pinks, creams, ochres, lavenders and minky browns is soothing to decorate with. You really can't go wrong with many close shades of this colour range. Think of a Californian pebbled beach of miles of various shades of grey – the image is somehow riveting.

My favourite use of close colour can be seen in shell grottoes with the restricted palette emphasizing the elegant forms of the rows of shells. Old shadow boxes of shells arranged in dazzling patterns have always caught my eye in antique shops. I made my own version for this room. As I arranged it, I was struck by how many colours exist in the simple fan shell – deep lavenders, hot corals, and delicious pinks and golds.

As one of the centrepieces for my shells and animals drawing room, I designed the large *Shells Rag Rug*. When selecting subjects for the rug, I had to choose strongly patterned, contrasting, and sharply defined shells. For them to stand out on the washy blue and

ABOVE: The shell pavilion at Goodwood Park in Sussex is a wonderful extravagance of shells in an interior. LEFT: This shell shadowbox displays a gorgeous range of restrained shell colours and shapes.

grey ground, they had to have areas of bright cream, yellow or pink. The fans atop the wavy yellow and duck-egg blue border serve to contain and edge the rug. It is amazing how little shading is needed on a shell to give a sense of roundness. Forms on rag rugs need to be fairly flat and simplified to read.

The needlepoint *Shell Chair* makes use of a wonderful seventeenth-century painting of a bower of shells by Jan van Kessel. The painting is featured in my book *Glorious Inspirations* and was also the basis for the *Shells and Turtles Carpet* on pages 44 and 45. The tawny Rembrandt ambers, rusts and deep velvety browns of the chair are pleasurable to work with and go so well with wood tones. The hint of pink and grey hues makes the chair harmonize beautifully with the pastel shades in this room.

My assistant Brandon Mably's first attempt at rug hooking produced the exuberant *Rooster Rag Rug*. He exaggerated the breast feathers with large stitches and did a very tight background to give a magnificent sense of dimension to the bird. If you think you can't draw, you should be encouraged to hear that Brandon has had no formal art training but just plunges into dealing with any design subject with amusing and amazing results.

A contemporary painting by Dutch artist Erno Trump was my model for the *Silky*

ABOVE: Boldly marked shells on the *Shells on Sand Cushion.*

the Cow Cushion and I love the placid black and whiteness of her. You could easily change the background colours and the tile border to suit any scheme you were designing for. Ochre grass and a pale yellow sky could be interesting with a pink and blue tile surround.

Once all the paintings, rag rugs and stitched panels were in place in this shells and animals interior, they seemed to dictate a smoky blue floor. The pink peeling table became part of the room treatment because it had just enough colour to bring out the hint of pink in the shells. The *Lobster* and *Crab Cushions* provide a sharp focus among all those soft tones in the room. The crab and lobster theme is one I did as a one-off needlepoint bag for my book *Glorious Needlepoint.* I got so many letters requesting a kit, that I decided to produce cushions of them separately (see page 157 for kit details).

Shells on Sand Cushion

Size of cushion

The finished cushion measures 51cm (20¼in) wide by 41cm (16¼in) tall.

Materials

- 10-mesh single- or double-thread canvas 66cm (26in) by 56cm (22in)
- APPLETON wool tapestry yarn in the 15 colours listed on page 41
- Size 18 tapestry needle
- 70cm (¾yd) of 90cm (36in) wide backing fabric and matching sewing thread
- 2m (2¼yd) of piping (filling) cord or ready-made cord (optional)
- 46cm (18in) zipper
- Cushion pad (pillow form) same size as finished cover or slightly larger

Key

A B C D E F G H I J K L M N O

Yarn colours and amounts

You will need Appleton wool tapestry yarn (10m/11yd skeins) in the following 15 colours and approximate amounts:

A	Brown-black	588	1 skein
B	Deep brown grounding	582	2 skeins
C	Dark golden brown	905	2 skeins
D	Mid chocolate	184	3 skeins
E	Putty grounding	983	4 skeins
F	Pale iron grey	961	15 skeins
G	Off white	992	6 skeins
H	Dark cornflower blue	463	1 skein
I	Mid cornflower blue	462	2 skeins
J	Pale cornflower blue	461	3 skeins
K	Terracotta	122	1 skein
L	Pale coral	861	2 skeins
M	Dark autumn yellow	479	1 skein
N	Mid autumn yellow	477	2 skeins
O	Light autumn yellow	474	2 skeins

Working the embroidery

The chart is 204 stitches wide and 164 stitches tall. Begin by marking the outline of the design on to your canvas and, if desired, dividing it into tens just like the charted design. Make a paper template of the design outline and set aside to use later as a guide for blocking.

Following the chart on left, work the embroidery in tent stitch, using one strand of Appleton wool tapestry yarn (see page 150 for tent stitch techniques). Work the shells first, leaving the background (pale iron grey, shade no. 961) until last.

Finishing the cushion cover

After the embroidery has been completed, block the canvas, using the paper template as your guide (see page 152).

Trim the canvas edges, leaving a seam allowance of 2cm (¾in).

Sew the zipper between two pieces of fabric for the cushion cover back as instructed on page 152.

If desired, cover the piping (filling) cord and pin to the needlepoint. Then join the front and back of the cover as described on page 152. If you are using a ready-made cord as a trimming, sew it on last.

ABOVE: The vigorous flow of multicoloured ground on the *Shells Rag Rug* called for strongly delineated shell forms.

Note: Each square on the grid represents 10cm (4in).

Shells Rag Rug

Size of rag rug

The finished rag rug measures 100cm (40in) wide by 165cm (66in) long.

Materials

- Piece of loose-weave hessian (burlap) at least 116cm (46in) by 179cm (70in)
- Variety of scrap fabrics for strips (see *Choosing the colours* above)
- Large rug hook
- 5.8m (6 1/4yd) of 6cm (2 1/2in) wide twilled carpet binding tape (optional)
- Strong thread for hemming

Choosing the colours

You will need scrap fabrics in a variety of colours and in a range of tones. Study the photograph of the rug for an idea of the types of colours to choose. Then look for scraps to fit into this scheme or to fit into your own original palette. (See page 147 for information on types of fabrics suitable for rag rugs.)

Transferring the design

Using a dressmaker's marking pen, mark the outer outline of the rug on to the right side of the hessian (burlap). The dimensions of the outer outline are shown on the rug design diagram. Allow at least 8cm (3in) of extra fabric all around the edge.

Following the rug diagram, transfer the rug design on to the right side of the fabric as instructed on page 148.

Preparing the rag strips

Cut some of the fabric scraps into strips 1.5cm (1/2in) to 2.5cm (1in) wide, depending on the thickness of the fabric. Cut only enough strips to provide a variety of tones and shades for working the first shell. Cut the remaining scraps only when you need them as the work progresses.

A detailed explanation of how to cut strips for rag rugs is given on page 148.

Hooking the rug

Before starting to hook the rug, read the hooking instructions on page 149.

Then begin the rug by working the individual shells at the centre of the design, using rag strips of the desired colour.

After completing the shells at the centre, work the border. Then work the fan shells around the border, leaving the shell background until last.

Finishing the rug

After the hooking has been completed, bind the edges of the hessian (burlap) if desired, then turn back the edges and work the hem, mitring the corners. Turn to page 149 for finishing instructions.

HALI

PREVIOUS PAGES: My *Shells and Turtles Carpet* (available as a needlepoint kit, see page 157) glows with Rembrandt golds and browns. ABOVE: The *Shells Waistcoat/Vest* was my first attempt at wearable needlepoint. RIGHT: The *Cat on Carpet Cushion*.

Geometric marquetry woodwork has always appealed to me in a big way. I love rich warm wood tones. It was my collection of boxes that acted as the spark for this second shells and animals interior treatment. Amber shells, marquetry, baskets, grasses and tortoiseshell cats make this a cosy room to curl up in with a book on a cold winter day.

I used brown parcel paper for the walls and had Brandon paint me a shell border in acrylics. When a white paper ground on the border proved too contrasty, he painted ochre and pinky-brown washes over it. Over the brown paper I hung an old French patchwork quilt and gathered country pots with deep amber glazes to enrich the colour scheme.

I bought the old screen with its warm brocade tones in Portobello flea market in the 1970s for only a few pounds and I have since often used it as a backdrop for my still lifes. The old tin trunk painted in mock wood grain also comes from Portobello market.

The voluminous creature in my *Turkey Rag Rug* decked out in his passionate finery is at home in all these warm colours. The rug was a joy to hook. I started on the body, not knowing what I would do for a background. I was then given some cloth in gorgeous shades of yellow. That range of yellow streaked with fleshy pinks gave a radiant autumn mood to the piece.

Tortoiseshell cats steel my heart with their swirly patterns. These patterns are a perfect texture to recreate in needlepoint. The organic fur markings on the cat in the *Cat on Cushion* needlepoint mix well with the patterns on the carpet cushion the cat lays on.

The design source for the knitted *Striped Cat Cushion* is a marquetry cat by the sixteenth-century Italian artist Fra' Raffaele da Brescia. The bold brown markings were ideal for knitting in contrasting yarns.

Turkey Rag Rug

Size of rag rug

The finished rag rug measures 88cm (35in) wide by 80cm (32in) tall.

Materials

- Piece of loose-weave hessian (burlap) at least 104cm (41in) by 96cm (38in)
- Variety of scrap fabrics for strips (see *Choosing the colours* below)
- Large rug hook
- 3.7m (4yd) of 6cm (2½in) wide twilled carpet binding tape (optional)
- Strong thread for hemming

Choosing the colours

You will need scrap fabrics in a variety of colours and in a range of tones. Study the photograph of the rug for an idea of the types of colours to choose. Then look for scraps to fit into this scheme or to fit into your own original palette. (See page 147 for information on types of fabrics suitable for rag rugs.)

Transferring the design

Using a dressmaker's marking pen, mark the outer outline of the rug on to the right side of the hessian (burlap). The dimensions of the outer outline are given above under *Size of rag rug* and are shown on the rug design diagram. Allow at least 8cm (3in) of extra fabric all around the edge.

Following the rug diagram, transfer the rug design on to the right side of the fabric as instructed on page 148.

Preparing the rag strips

Cut some of the fabric scraps into strips 1.5cm (½in) to 2.5cm (1in) wide, depending on the thickness of the fabric. Cut only enough strips to provide a variety of tones and shades for working a small section of the turkey. Cut the remaining scraps only when you need them as the work progresses.

A detailed explanation of how to cut strips for rag rugs is given on page 148.

RIGHT: The amount of detail and the range of colour one can achieve with rough rags is amazing. ABOVE: This was the Victorian model for my *Turkey Rag Rug.*

Hooking the rug

Before starting to hook the rug, read the hooking instructions on page 149.

Then begin the rug by working the turkey, using rag strips of the desired colour. (As a guideline, the rug diagram indicates some of the colours used on the original *Turkey Rag Rug.*)

After completing the turkey, work a single row of loops all around the outer outline of the rug. Then work the ground below the turkey in wavy horizontal rows of loops. Next work two more rows of loops in contrasting colours around the outer edge of the sky. Lastly, work the sky in slightly curvy horizontal rows of loops.

Finishing the rug

After the hooking has been completed, bind the edges of the hessian (burlap) if desired, then turn back the edges and work the hem, mitring the corners. Turn to page 149 for finishing instructions.

Note: Each square on the grid represents 10cm (4in).

Striped Cat Cushion

Size of cushion

The finished cushion measures 51cm (20½in) wide by 43cm (17½in) tall. The knitted centre square measures approximately 46cm (18½in) by 38cm (15½in) excluding the check border.

Materials

• Rowan *Lightweight DK* (25g/1oz hanks) in the following 6 colours:

A	Rust	27	2 hanks
B	Brick	77	1 hank
C	Gold	72	3 hanks
D	Light mustard	402	1 hank
E	Dusky salmon	86	1 hank
F	Light brown	87	3 hanks
G	Ochre	9	3 hanks

• Rowan *Donegal Lambswool Tweed* (25g/1oz hanks) in the following 2 colours:

H	Bark	475	3 hanks
J	Pickle	483	3 hanks

• One pair each of 4½mm (US size 7) and 5mm (US size 8) knitting needles
• Small piece of scrap fabric for backing the knitting
• 70cm (¾yd) of 90cm (36in) wide fabric for cushion cover back and matching sewing thread
• 45cm (18in) zipper
• Cushion pad (pillow form) same size as finished cover or slightly larger

Knitting stitch gauge

18 sts and 27 rows to 10cm (4in) measured over st st using yarn doubled and 5mm (US size 8) knitting needles.
19 sts and 25 rows to 10cm (4in) measured over pattern using yarn doubled and 5mm (US size 8) knitting needles.

Special notes

Note that the knitting yarns are used double throughout. The yarns are used in various combinations: for example, AA means 2 strands of yarn A used together, CG means one strand of yarn C and one strand of yarn G used together, and so on.

ABOVE: A hard marquetry source was reproduced in the soft texture of knitting for my *Striped Cat* design.

When working the colourwork pattern, use a mixture of the Fair Isle and intarsia techniques. Use the intarsia method for working the background, using a separate length of yarn for each area of the striped background and linking one colour to the next by twisting them around each other on WS where they meet to avoid holes. Use the Fair Isle method for working the cat (and the check border), carrying the colour not in use loosely across the WS of the cat and weaving it in every 3 or 4 sts to avoid long loose ends.
Read chart from right to left for k (RS odd-numbered) rows and from left to right for p (WS even-numbered) rows.

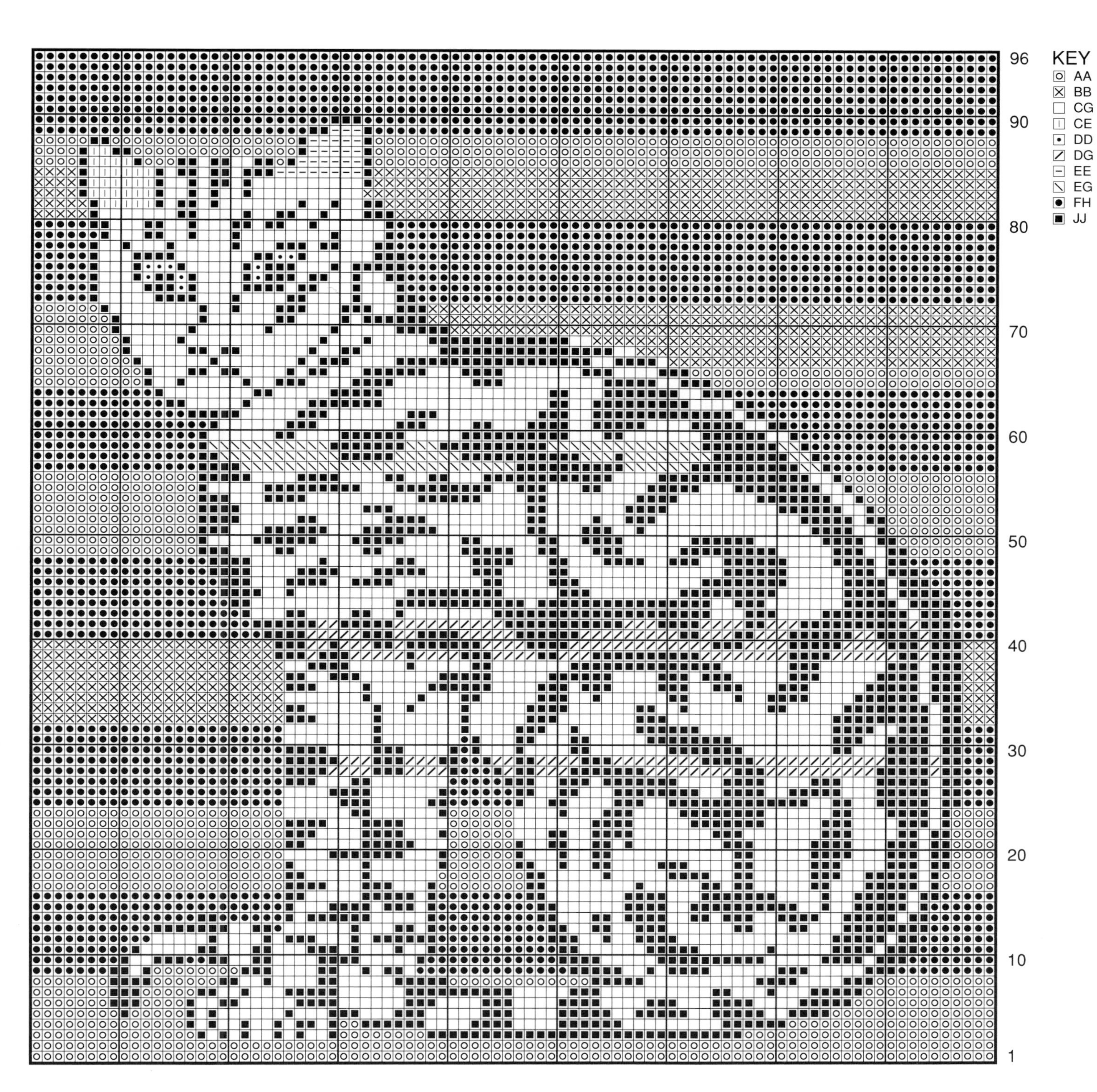

Charted cat design

Using larger needles and 2 strands of yarn A, cast on 88 sts.

Beg with a k row, work 96 rows in st st following chart for colourwork pattern (see special notes on previous page for how to work patterns in the Fair Isle and intarsia techniques), so ending with a p row.

Using FH, cast (bind) off loosely.

Press the finished piece lightly on WS with a damp cloth and a warm iron.

Check border

With RS facing and using smaller needles and CG and FH, pick up and knit 88 sts along the cast (bound) off edge as follows:

With CG pick up and k one st in each of first 4 sts, [with FH pick up and k one st in each of next 8 sts, with CG pick up and k one st in each of next 8 sts] 5 times, with FH pick up and k one st in each of last 4 sts. (88 sts)

Work top border as follows:

ABOVE: This late seventeenth-century Delft jug is deliciously witty and would translate into any media.

1st row (WS) With FH p into front and back of first st, p3, [with CG p8, with FH p8] 5 times, with CG p2, p into front and back of next st, p1. (90 sts)
2nd row With CG k into front and back of first st, k4, [with FH k8, with CG k8] 5 times, with FH k3, k into front and back of next st, k1. (92 sts)
Rep first and 2nd rows once more, then rep first row once, so ending with a p row. (98 sts)
Using FH, knit one row.
Using FH, cast (bind) off knitwise.
With RS facing and using smaller needles and CG and FH, pick up and knit 88 sts evenly along the cast-on edge as for top border.
Work 6 rows as for top border.
With RS facing and using smaller needles and CG and FH, pick up and knit 74 sts evenly along one of side edges as follows:
With CG pick up and k 5 sts, [with FH pick up and k 8 sts, with CG pick up and k 8 sts] 4 times, with FH pick up and k 5 sts. (74 sts)
Work side border as follows:
1st row (WS) With FH p into front and back of first st, p4, [with CG p8, with FH p8] 4 times, with CG p3, p into front and back of next st, p1. (76 sts)
2nd row With CG k into front and back of first st, k5, [with FH k8, with CG k8] 4 times, with FH k4, k into front and back of next st, k1. (78 sts)
Rep first and 2nd rows once more, then rep first row once, so ending with a p row. (84 sts)
Using FH, knit one row.
Using FH, cast (bind) off knitwise.
Work remaining side border in same way.

Finishing the cushion cover

Join mitred corner seams. Then press border lightly on WS.
Cut a piece of scrap fabric the same size as the knitting plus a 1.5cm (½in) seam allowance all around the edge.
With the wrong sides facing each other, pin the knitting to the centre of this piece of fabric. Then sew the two layers together, working small running stitches very close to the edge of the knitting.
Sew the zipper between two pieces of fabric for the cushion cover back and join the front and back of the cover as instructed on page 152, catching the edge of the knitting into the seam.

faces

Carousels and gigantic laughing heads at fairgrounds were probably my first encounters with the delightful faces theme, and they have kept me aware of its spell-binding qualities ever since. Cultures as diverse as those of Italy and China use faces with great humour and style as design elements in gardens, on buildings and for objects in interiors. When I first went to Italy I was amazed to see faces used in monumental architecture. Thinking of Italian ornament conjures up for me the famous Mouth of Truth at the church of Santa Maria in Cosmedin in Rome, a huge moonlike carved face that featured in the film *Roman Holiday.* In Italy for sheer drama there are also decorative stone faces with gaping mouths that serve as doorways.

If you look at the human physiognomy in the way a decorative artist does, you will see why it is so infinitely malleable as a vessel for shape and colour – and always so captivating. It has two eyes which shine out like jewels; an expressive mouth; a nose that can be comically red, pointed, flat or crooked; and hair that can take on a wide variety of shapes, and can be curled or straight, ash white, deep red or raven black. This vivid countenance can then be further enhanced by being topped with clown-like baldness or crowned with any number of hats – even one sprouting leaves and flowers! The possibilities

LEFT: It delights me the way the *Faces Waistcoat/Vest,* the masks and the face cushions merge with my collage screen. OVERLEAF: Playing with stripes, I created a circus tent of a room for my many faces designs.

GIVE
and see your

ABOVE: Self-portrait by Belgian artist James Ensor.
LEFT: The painting inspired my *Faces Waistcoat/Vest.*

exist for any mood or scheme you can dream up. Small wonder that we encounter the face motif time and again in ornament around the world.

Finding faces in unexpected places such as walking sticks, marble fireplaces, or door knockers always gives me a shiver of delight, so why not a whole room with faces everywhere! Because faces hark back to circuses in my memory, I envisioned my interior from the start in lively contrasting Victorian pastels, with a chalky softness to them.

With circus tents in bold two-colour stripes in mind and wanting to include animal faces in the menagerie, I designed the jaunty *Cat with Ruff Cushion.* Then looking for a classic head to needlepoint, I came across a portrait of a woman that hangs in the National Gallery in London. The face in this composition is framed in tantalizing creamy white folds of cloth. These muted medieval tones contain a cool presence of their own and I thought they would work well as a highlight in my schema.

Because of my fascination with faces, I have always been drawn to Victorian collage screens covered with figurative images. During the time I was working on my faces room, I did a lecture tour in the United States and Canada. While there I saw a collage screen with large ladies' portraits at the top of each panel of the screen. Immediately after seeing this I was seized with the desire to create one in a similar vein, covered with torsos and faces. Once I got the bug to do it, there was no stopping me. In all twelve cities I visited on my tour, I combed every bookstore for stimulating reproductions of the painted face. These theme screens could be done with any subject. Imagine an animal collage or china pots – or houses.

As I continued to gather props for my room, I spotted bold two-colour stripe fabric every-

ABOVE: I spotted this black and white radiating stripe ground in an old ad and bagged it for my bright *Masks Cushion*.

ABOVE: Faces used as architectural detail always intrigue me. This highly coloured one emerging from dense detail on a column in the Himalayas is a beaut! TOP: My *Victorian Faces Collage Screen.*

where. The gold and terracotta chair fabric and carpet went so well with the vivid purple and gold stripe cotton I found on a trip to India. With all this joyous stripiness it seemed only natural to divide the walls into a huge series of circus tent stripes. I chose deeper blue and ochre gold for the stripe at first but felt that would be a bit oppressive. This pale amber gold and Gauloise blue keep the mood light and optimistic to my eye. Its dynamic contrast makes a powerful accent. The striped pots on the table complete the picture.

Combing Camden Lock market for masks to further my theme, I was thrilled to find a shop with a door covered in bright Indonesian masks. The chalky glow of the banana yellow, candy pink, and musty blues of these masks fitted right into the burgeoning faces room. I used the masks for the border of painted bowers and also as models for the *Masks Cushion* needlepoint.

Along with the jam-packed *Victorian Faces Screen,* I designed another intricate confection of faces for a needlepoint waistcoat/vest. Although the idea was inspired by Ensor's well-known painting, an amazing array of sources were used for this diverse group – portraits on postcards, details from famous paintings, dolls, and old Roman frescos. I did not hesitate to choose animal as well as human physiognomies. A cat and dog sit comfortably on the needlepoint alongside Queen Elizabeth I and George Washington. It is all grist to the mill!

Victorian Faces Collage Screen

Materials

- Screen or other foundation for collage
- Strong paper glue
- Selection of face cutouts from magazines, books and postcards
- Ochre acrylic and paint brush (optional)

Applying the collage cutouts

Starting at the top of one section of the screen, arrange a few of the collage cutouts. Stand back to study the arrangement, then glue these first pieces in place. Continue in this way, working downwards. (See page 153 for more detailed instructions for collage techniques.)

Cover each section of the screen in the same way, but varying the pattern.

Finishing the screen

If desired, glaze the collage with an ochre acrylic wash for an antique finish.

ABOVE: A ruff is such a good frame for a face. It really sets off the perky eyes and ears on the feline face of the *Cat with Ruff Cushion*. I designed the background of soft radiating stripes to go with the striped fabrics and walls in the room.

Cat with Ruff Cushion

Size of cushion

The finished cushion measures 41cm (16 1/4in) wide by 40cm (15 3/4in) tall.

Materials

- 10-mesh single- or double-thread canvas 56cm (22in) square
- ANCHOR wool tapestry yarn in the 12 colours listed on the right
- Size 18 tapestry needle
- 70cm (3/4yd) of 90cm (36in) wide backing fabric and matching sewing thread for finishing the cushion cover
- 1.8m (2yd) of piping (filling) cord or ready-made cord (optional)
- 35cm (14in) zipper
- Cushion pad (pillow form) same size as finished cover or slightly larger

Yarn colours and amounts

You will need Anchor wool tapestry yarn (10m/11yd skeins) in the following 12 colours and approximate amounts:

A	Deep mink	9682	1 skein
B	Dark nutmeg	9450	1 skein

C	Mid sand	9526	1 skein
D	Light sand	9524	1 skein
E	Pale autumn gold	8056	1 skein
F	Dark moss green	9214	1 skein
G	Bright leaf green	9194	5 skeins
H	Damson	8504	5 skeins
I	Mid sky blue	8818	1 skein
J	Light sky blue	8814	1 skein
K	Pale cloud grey	8702	1 skein
L	Off white	8006	3 skeins

Working the embroidery

The chart for this cushion is 164 stitches wide and 158 stitches tall. Before beginning the embroidery, mark the outline of the design on to your needlepoint canvas and, if desired, divide it into tens just like the charted design. Make a paper template of the design outline and set aside to use later as a guide for blocking.

Following the chart on the right, work the embroidery in tent stitch, using one strand of Anchor wool tapestry yarn (see page 150 for instructions for the various tent stitch techniques). Work the cat and ruff first, leaving the striped background (bright leaf green and damson, shade nos. 9194 and 8504) until last.

Finishing the cushion cover

After the embroidery has been completed, block the needlepoint canvas, using the paper template as your guide (see page 152 for blocking instructions).

Trim the canvas edges, leaving a seam allowance of 2cm (3/4in).

Using the zipper foot on your sewing machine, or stitching by hand, sew the zipper between two pieces of backing fabric for the cushion cover back as instructed on page 152.

If desired, cover the piping (filling) cord with fabric cut on the bias and pin it to the needlepoint. Then join the needlepoint front and the fabric back of the cover as described on page 152. If you are using a ready-made cord as a trimming, sew it to the completed cover, tucking the ends into a small opening in the seam.

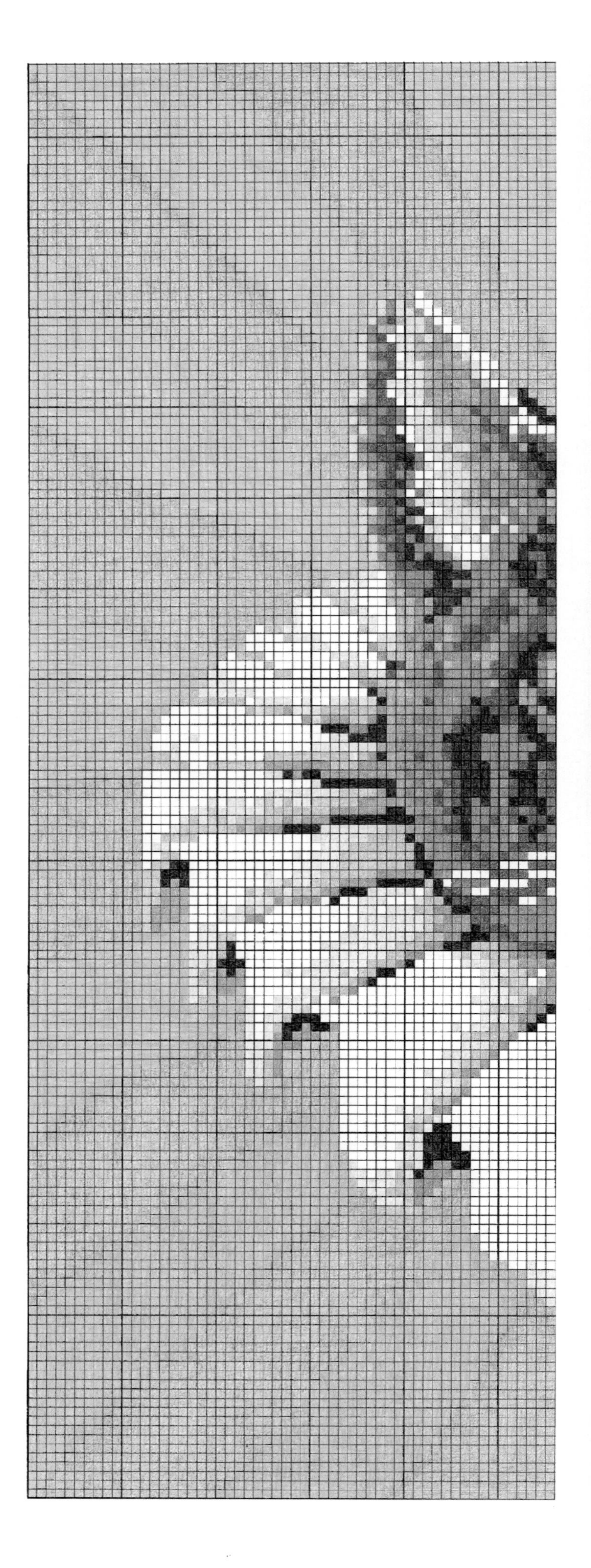

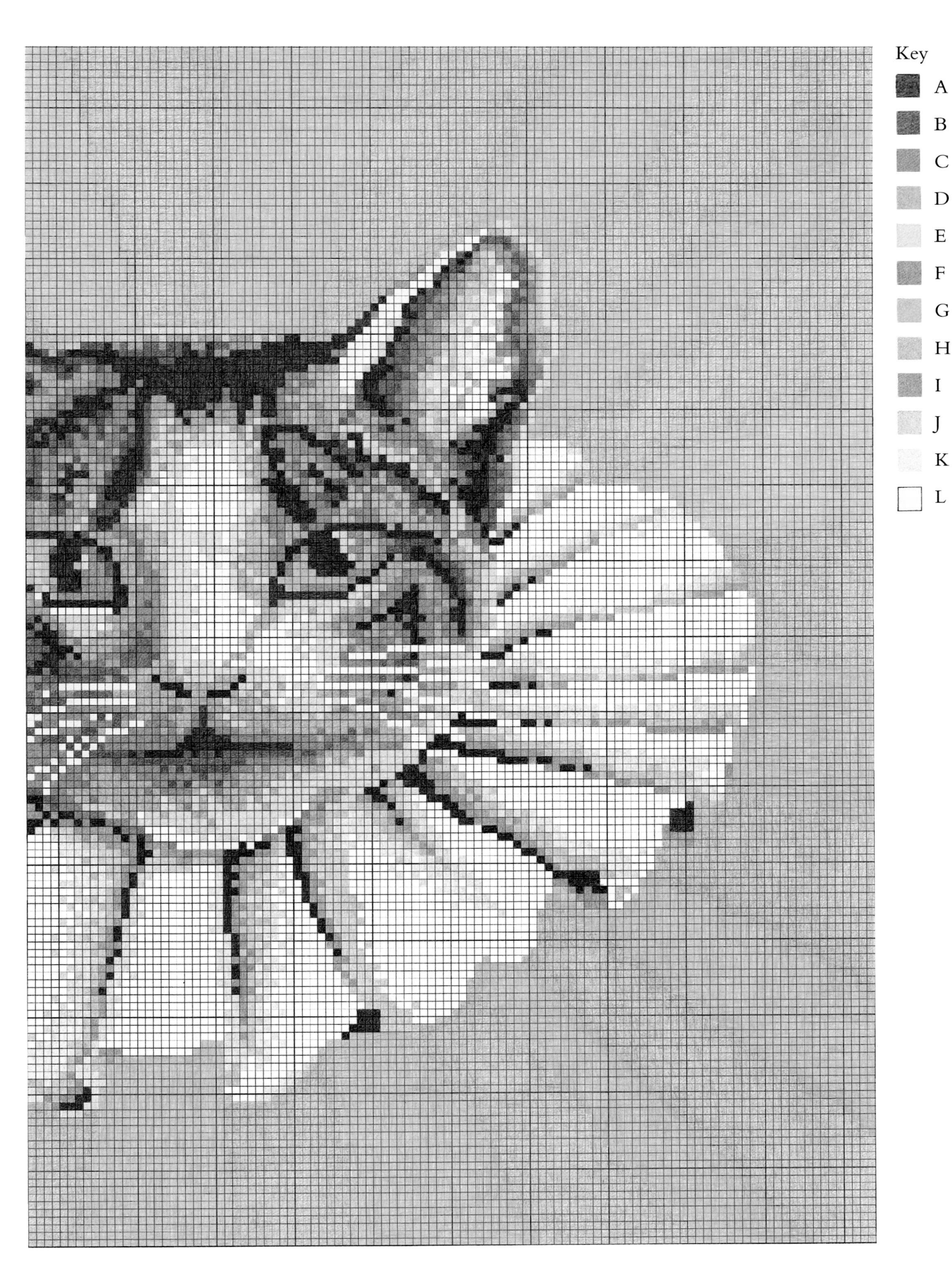
Key
A
B
C
D
E
F
G
H
I
J
K
L

Key
A
B
C
D
E
F
G
H
I
J
K
L
M
N

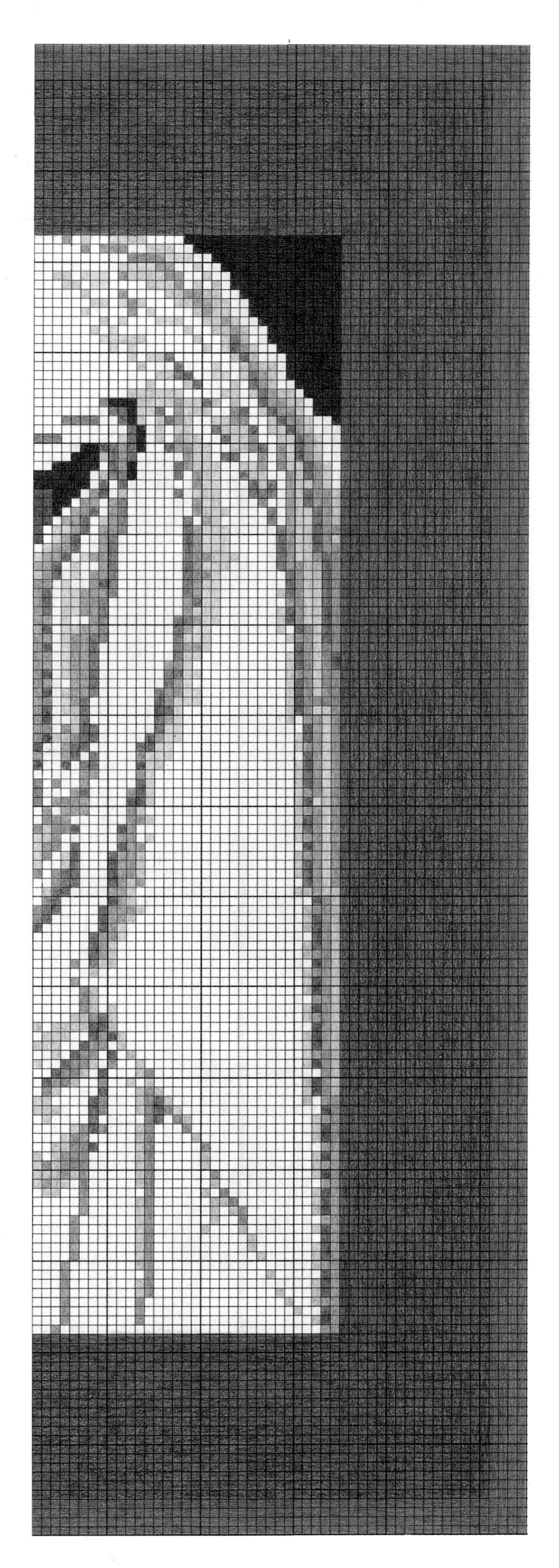

ABOVE: As I worked this design, I was excited to see the face on my *Medieval Face* needlepoint cushion come to life, despite the restricted palette.

Medieval Face Cushion

Size of cushion

The finished cushion measures 39cm (15½in) wide by 41cm (16¼in) tall.

Materials

- 10-mesh single- or double-thread canvas 56cm cm (22in) square
- ANCHOR wool tapestry yarn in the 14 colours listed on page 66
- Size 18 tapestry needle
- 70cm (¾yd) of 90cm (36in) wide backing fabric and matching sewing thread
- 1.8m (2yd) of piping (filling) cord or ready-made cord (optional)
- 33cm (13in) zipper
- Cushion (pillow form) same size as finished cover or slightly larger

Yarn colours and amounts

You will need Anchor wool tapestry yarn (10m/11yd skeins) in the following 14 colours and approximate amounts:

A	Deep ocean blue	8840	1 skein
B	Dark grey	9794	1 skein
C	Dark ocean blue	8836	3 skeins
D	Cathedral blue	8786	2 skeins
E	Pale cloud grey	8704	2 skeins
F	White	8000	9 skeins
G	Mid mink	9678	11 skeins
H	Light mink	9676	1 skein
I	Pale mink	9674	1 skein
J	Damson	8504	1 skein
K	Pale lavender	8542	2 skeins
L	Bronze flesh	9510	1 skein
M	Pale peach	8296	1 skein
N	Off white	8006	1 skein

Working the embroidery

The chart is 155 stitches wide and 164 stitches tall. Begin by marking the outline of the design on to your canvas and, if desired, dividing it into tens just like the charted design. Make a paper template of the design outline and set aside to use later as a guide for blocking.

Following the chart on pages 64 and 65, work the embroidery in tent stitch, using one strand of Anchor wool tapestry yarn (see page 150 for tent stitch techniques). Leaving the background until last, work the face first, then the veil. Note that the 'white' used on the veil is shade no. 8000 and the 'white' used on the face and the eyes is shade no. 8006.

Finishing the cushion cover

After the embroidery has been completed, block the needlepoint canvas, using the paper template as your guide (see page 152).

Trim the canvas edges, leaving a seam allowance of 2cm (¾in).

Sew the zipper between two pieces of fabric for the cushion cover back as instructed on page 152.

If desired, cover the piping (filling) cord and pin to the needlepoint. Then join the front and back of the cover as described on page 152. If you are using a ready-made cord as a trimming, sew it to the completed cover, tucking the ends into a small opening in the seam.

ABOVE: Shell face from Basildon Park, Berkshire. TOP: Brandon Mably's green man rag rug. RIGHT: My *Stone Head Cushion*. TOP RIGHT: Inventive use of faces in a sixteenth-century Valois tapestry, Uffizi, Florence.

Needlepoint is a superb vehicle for portraits. I'm sure its easier than painting people. I was worried about being able to get a realistic sense of features in stitches but find it is really quite an accurate media for portraiture. To get more detail into small faces like these, you should work on a fine 14-mesh canvas.

Try working a tent stitch face following your favourite photo and see how you fare. A chair or rug covered with family and friends would be the ultimate conversation piece! It would also be wonderful to do portraits of your family stretching back to the ancestors in the form of a waistcoat, cushion

or wall hanging. Needlepoint is so much more lively a texture than old sepia photos!

Of course, sepia or black, white and grey tones have a definite beauty in the right situation. I've seen black and white photo portraits reproduced in weaving creating an eerie excitement. I was thinking of that when I stitched the *Stone Head Cushion* from a photograph in a magazine. This classic carved head with its broken nose and the dynamic crack down its centre was quite appetizing to stitch. I tried to get all the subtle suggested tones into the shadows while keeping the strong outline.

We photographed the *Stone Head Cushion* apart from our pastel room because its monochrome would have looked a little dingy there. Sitting on the stone step against a mossy gothic door it looks really dynamic.

ABOVE: The effectiveness of grey tones on the brutal face of my *Stone Head Cushion* made me want to see black and white photo portraits done in needlepoint.

Stone Head Cushion

Size of cushion

The finished cushion measures 39cm (15 ¼in) wide by 41cm (16in) tall.

Materials

- 10-mesh single- or double-thread canvas 54cm (21in) square
- ANCHOR wool tapestry yarn in the 14 colours listed on page 70
- Size 18 tapestry needle
- 70cm (¾yd) of 90cm (36in) wide backing fabric and matching sewing thread
- 1.8m (2yd) of piping (filling) cord or ready-made cord (optional)
- 30cm (12in) zipper
- Cushion pad (pillow form) same size as finished cover or slightly larger

Yarn colours and amounts

You will need Anchor wool tapestry yarn (10m/11yd skeins) in the following 14

Key
A
B
C
D
E
F
G
H
I
J
K
L
M
N

colours and approximate amounts:

A	Deep sea green	8906	3 skeins
B	Grey green	9066	4 skeins
C	Gobelin green	8876	2 skeins
D	Dark chocolate	9662	2 skeins
E	Medium brown	9638	3 skeins
F	Light chocolate	9654	3 skeins
G	Light khaki	9324	2 skeins
H	Pale putty fawn	9362	2 skeins
I	Deep priest grey	9768	2 skeins
J	Dark priest grey	9764	5 skeins
K	Medium granite	9776	5 skeins
L	Light grey	9786	8 skeins
M	Pale grey	9784	3 skeins
N	Pale granite	9772	3 skeins

Working the embroidery

The chart is 154 stitches wide and 162 stitches tall. Begin by marking the outline of the design on to your canvas and, if desired, dividing it into tens just like the charted design. Make a paper template of the design outline and set aside to use later as a guide for blocking after completing the work.

Following the chart on pages 68 and 69, work the embroidery in tent stitch, using one strand of Anchor wool tapestry yarn (see page 150 for nstructions for the various tent stitch techniques).

Finishing the cushion cover

After the embroidery has been completed, block the canvas, using the paper template as your guide (see page 152).

Trim the canvas edges, leaving a seam allowance of 2cm (3/4in).

Sew the zipper between two pieces of fabric for the cushion cover back as instructed on page 152.

If desired, cover the piping (filling) cord and pin to the needlepoint. Then join the front and back of the cover as described on page 152. If you are using a ready-made cord as a trimming, sew it to the completed cover, tucking the ends into a small opening in the seam.

mosaics

Fragments of pattern in any medium fascinate me. Patchwork quilts, collages and mosaics all have a mysterious charm because in them familiar motifs are juxtaposed to create unexpectedly fresh arrangements. Patchwork often makes use of quite unattractive materials to create very handsome and original patterns. Even harsh black and white motifs or vulgar fifties patterns

take on an oriental intricacy when fragmented and forced into a geometric structure.

Mosaic creates the same sense of newness but uses the harder surface of porcelain or pottery. It can be very bold when worked in solid colours, or kaleidoscopic when composed of decorated china or tiles. A combination of these two styles can be very exciting, the patterned porcelain appearing that much more intricate against the plain solid shards.

The king of mosaic for me is the Spanish architect Antonio Gaudí. His use of mosaic in parks and on buildings has such outstanding personality. One of the tricks I noticed he employed was to take large geometric or flowery tiles that were quite stiffly symmetrical, smash them to pieces only to reassemble the bits so they add up to a totally fresh abstract tile.

LEFT: Small dishes and pot covers make good centres for these circular mosaic wall plates. OVERLEAF: What I wanted for my garden terrace was a sunny Mediterranean feel with a predominance of blue and white, and pink and yellow.

ABOVE: Antonio Gaudí's mosaic bench in Parc Güell in Barcelona is my world favourite mosaic object and a huge influence. LEFT: Detail of Gaudí's bench. FAR LEFT: *Broken Tile Cushion* inspired by the bench.

Gaudí was a master at reinventing architectural forms, and the marriage of colour, pattern and form on his famous serpentine bench in the Parc Güell in Barcelona is on my list of world wonders. This brilliant essay on Spanish tiles, all rearranged by a spontaneous masterly eye, snakes through this charming park. I spent a few exotic hours studying it on my first visit and have been inspired by it ever since.

What I wanted for my garden terrace was a sunny Mediterranean feel – pink, yellow, and blue and white were my predominant colours. You can see that these are Gaudí's colours for his serpentine bench in Parc Güell. Seeing how he and so many other designers from Mediterranean cultures have made jolly spaces to live and entertain in *al fresco,* I thought I'd do the same. I often do my work outdoors, and I love outdoor cafés, even on winter days. There is no reason why you shouldn't decorate an outdoor environment with as much attention as you would an interior. Some people do it with plants and flowers, but I like the dancing vitality of mosaics outdoors, and they only get better as they age and weather.

There are many moods that can be achieved with this colourful medium. Because I love bronzed and darker plants in my garden I have covered Victorian chimney pots with dark green, plum, cobalt blue, and even black and dark brown broken tiles and plates, creating a smouldering mood. For a really dazzling effect broken mirror could be used, but this is probably too glarey for the

ABOVE: The *Mosaic Collage Screen* is a collection of wallpaper, postcards and magazine cuttings on brown paper (see page 81).

outdoors. I did see a stunning mosque in Iran which had an interior covered floor to ceiling in mosaic mirror – the mirror pieces turned one candle into 5,000 twinkling lights!

I tried to create a dappled mosaic texture on as many surfaces as possible in my mosaic terrace. I covered tables, window surrounds, mirror frames, chimney pots, metal plates and a flower jug with fragments of patterned china. These mosaics could be rearranged at will to change the mood from time to time.

Often in antique shops I come across old Victorian mosaic pots with dark brown grout oozing out between very jolly bits of china. They are almost always wildly expensive, so I decided to have a go at making my own. I bought a cheap but nicely shaped pot, applied tile adhesive and covered it with medium to small size bits of broken china, bordering the base with old clay pipe stems. (See page 153 for mosaic techniques.)

Adding to my scheme, I collaged a folding screen with wallpaper fragments on brown wrapping paper panels, and hooked the *Mosaic Rag Rug*. To achieve a party-like atmosphere, I painted the paving stones of the terrace with washes of pastel acrylic. Of course, you could lay stone fragments with bits of broken patterned tiles sprinkled throughout for a more permanent completion of the scene.

A Dutch friend, Robert, left me a stunning collection of blue and white porcelain fragments that he had collected for years on his travels. I painted them in gratitude to his generous gift and went on to base a needlepoint, then a Designers Guild furnishing fabric on the painting. A yellow colourway of the *Shards* fabric is featured here, but it comes in several other colourways as well. The *Mosaic Pieces Cushion* needlepoint on my mosaic terrace is large enough to adapt as a chair seat.

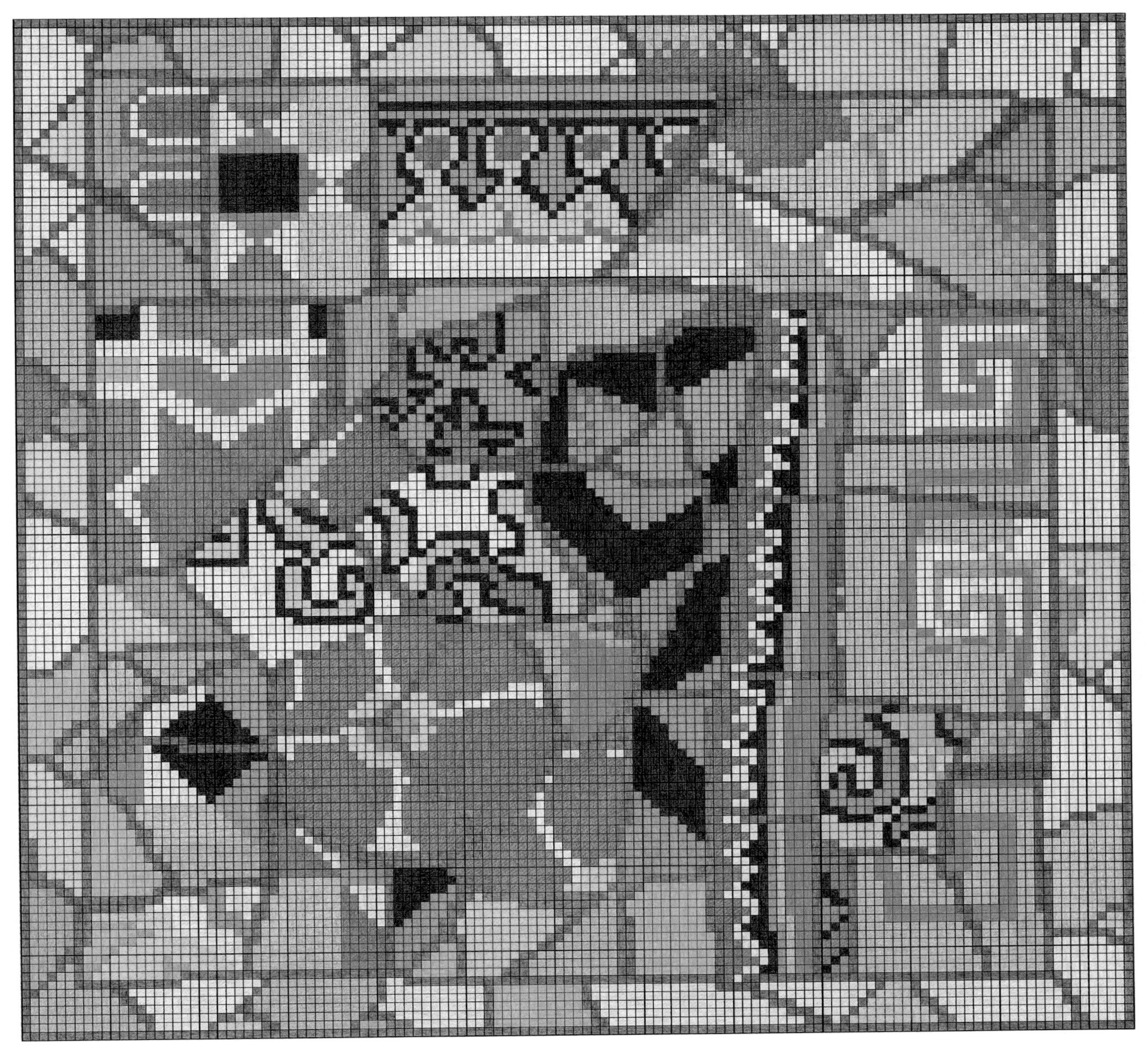

Key

A B C D E F G H I J K L M

Broken Tile Cushion

Size of cushion

The finished needlepoint cushion measures approximately 42cm (16 1/2in) wide by 41cm (16in) tall.

Materials

- 7- to 8-mesh interlock canvas 56cm (22in) square
- PATERNA/YAN *Persian Yarn* in the 13 colours listed on page 81
- Size 16 tapestry needle
- 70cm (3/4yd) of 90cm (36in) wide backing fabric and matching sewing thread
- 1.8m (2yd) of piping (filling) cord or ready-made cord (optional)
- 35cm (14in) zipper
- Cushion pad (pillow form) same size as finished cover or slightly larger

Yarn colours and amounts

You will need Paterna/yan Persian Yarn (7.4m/8yd skeins) in the following 13

colours and approximate amounts:

A	Deep coffee brown	420	5 skeins
B	Mid beige brown	462	9 skeins
C	Light fawn brown	405	5 skeins
D	Pale beige brown	465	10 skeins
E	Copper	862	2 skeins
F	Mid butterscotch	701	5 skeins
G	Light autumn yellow	726	5 skeins
H	Mid hunter green	612	3 skeins
I	Light pine green	663	2 skeins
J	Pale spring green	635	3 skeins
K	Mid ice blue	552	3 skeins
L	Light plum	324	3 skeins
M	American beauty pink	904	4 skeins

Working the embroidery

The chart is 125 stitches wide and 121 stitches tall. Begin by marking the outline of the design on to your canvas and, if desired, dividing it into tens just like the charted design. Make a paper template of the design outline and set aside to use for blocking.

Following the chart, work the needlepoint in tent stitch, using three strands of Paterna/yan Persian Yarn (see page 150 for tent stitch techniques). Work the mosaic outlines in mid beige brown (shade no. 462) before beginning to fill in the mosaic colours.

ABOVE: *Mosaic Collage Screen.* LEFT: My painting inspired the fabric and the *Mosaic Pieces Cushion.*

Finishing the cushion cover

After the embroidery has been completed, block the canvas, using the paper template as your guide (see page 152).

Trim the canvas edges, leaving a seam allowance of 2cm (3/4in).

Sew the zipper between two pieces of fabric for the cushion cover back as instructed on page 152.

If desired, cover the piping (filling) cord and pin to the needlepoint. Then join the front and back of the cover as described on page 152. If you are using a ready-made cord as a trimming, sew it to the completed cover, tucking the ends into the seam.

Mosaic Collage Screen

Materials

- Screen or other foundation for collage
- Brown wrapping paper for collage base
- Strong paper glue
- Selection of coloured patterns from magazines, wallpaper and postcards
- Ochre acrylic and paint brush (optional)

Applying the collage cutouts

Glue brown wrapping paper to each section of the screen.

Cut the patterned paper scraps into triangular and trapezoidal shapes.

Starting at the top of one section of the screen, arrange a few of these collage cutouts as desired. Stand back to study the arrangement, then glue these first pieces in place. Continue in this way, working downwards. (See page 153 for more instructions for collage.) Cover each section of the screen in the same way, but varying the pattern.

Finishing the screen

If desired, glaze the entire collage screen with an ochre acrylic wash.

ABOVE: Occasional stripes give a lively rhythm to the rag rug.

Mosaic Rag Rug

Size of rag rug

The finished rag rug measures 78cm (31in) wide by 120cm (48in) long.

Materials

- Piece of loose-weave hessian (burlap) at least 94cm (37in) by 134cm (53in)
- Variety of scrap fabrics for strips (see *Choosing the colours* below)
- Large rug hook
- 4.3m ($4\frac{3}{4}$yd) of 6cm ($2\frac{1}{2}$in) wide twilled carpet binding tape (optional)
- Strong thread for hemming

Choosing the colours

You will need scrap fabrics in a variety of colours and in a range of tones. Study the photograph of the rug for an idea of the types of colours to choose. Then look for scraps to fit into this scheme or to fit into your own original palette. (See rag rug techniques on page 147 for detailed information on collecting the types of fabrics suitable for making rag rugs.)

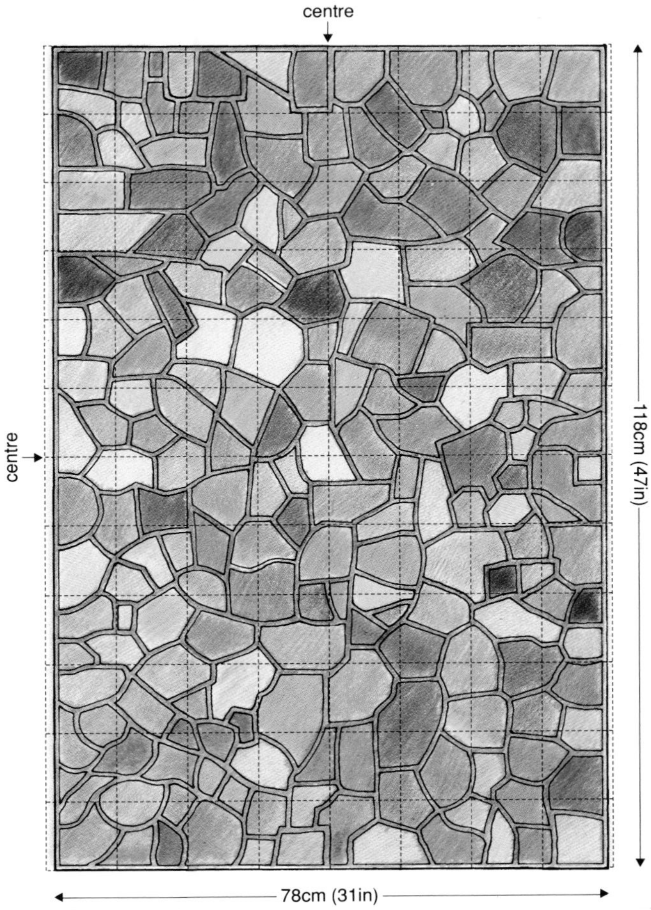

centre

centre

118cm (47in)

78cm (31in)

Note: Each square on the grid represents 10cm (4in).

Transferring the design

Using a dressmaker's marking pen, mark the outer outline of the rug on to the right side of the hessian (burlap). The dimensions of the outer outline are given under *Size of rag rug* and are shown on the rug design diagram. Allow at least 8cm (3in) of extra fabric all around the edge.

Following the rug diagram, transfer the rug design on to the right side of the fabric as instructed on page 148, or draw your own random mosaic shapes directly on to the fabric.

Preparing the rag strips

Cut some of the fabric scraps into strips 1.5cm ($\frac{1}{2}$in) to 2.5cm (1in) wide, depending on the thickness of the fabric. Cut only enough strips for working a section of the mosaic outline. Cut the remaining scraps only when you need them as the work progresses.

A detailed explanation of how to cut strips for rag rugs is given on page 148.

Hooking the rug

Before starting to hook the rug, read the hooking instructions on page 149.

Then begin the rug by working the mosaic outlines, using rag strips of the desired colour. (As a guideline, the rug diagram on the left indicates some of the colours used on the original *Mosaic Rag Rug*. Follow the photograph of the rag rug for further colour ideas.)

After completing the outlines, fill in the shapes, working some in solid colours, some in stripes, some in squares, some with dots, and some shaded, as desired.

Finishing the rug

After the hooking has been completed, bind the edges of the hessian (burlap) if desired, then turn back the edges and work the hem, mitring the corners. Turn to page 149 for finishing instructions.

ABOVE: Many mirrors give this tiny space an amazing depth. RIGHT: Brutal heaven? The pastel tiles of Watts Towers. FAR RIGHT: Fragments arranged as mosaic, a fresh look to the old theme of blue and white.

Attempting to decorate a bathroom in my assistant Brandon's little terraced house in Rye, I was presented with a problem often encountered in small flats. The bathroom was a tiny space that had to accommodate a basin, toilet, bath and the storage of linen and toiletries, while being a room visited several times a day by everyone in the house. The problem was how to make it appealing and not the claustrophobic closet it threatened to be.

I had seen a display of mirrors in a Vietnamese friend's bathroom and noted how spacious it made the place look; it was at the same time a jolly arrangement of shapes. The little mirrors for this bathroom were all purchased in junk shops around Rye at very reasonable prices.

The walls of the bathroom were originally white with pink tiles around the toilet, bath and sink. I chipped out the pink tiles and broke them down to reassemble with lots of broken plates and other tiles. It was amazing

how much material a large panel like this absorbed. When I was clearly running out of mosaic, I would walk into Rye to hit junk shops and the inevitable rummage sales to purchase cheap saucers, plates and old tiles to break and add to the arrangement. Bold patterned plates looked best. The ochre polka dots and navy and white patterns worked successfully with the bright yellow and pink constants. The bathroom is now a room of discovery because each time you visit, you spot a new area of detail to study.

ABOVE: The mosaic pot that was the inspiration for the *Mosaic Slippers* rests on a Rupert Spira striped sink. (For slippers available as needlepoint kits see pages 112 and 142.)

One of the great heroes of my childhood was an immigrant engineer called Simon Rodia who settled in Watts, on the edge of Los Angeles. For years he constructed a series of towers that resembled a great ship with masts (see pages 8 and 84). He concreted every inch of the steel framework and embedded broken tiles, plates, marbles, shells, etc. into the concrete. These Watts Towers delighted everyone who encountered them either in the flesh or in the photos accompanying the many articles and books written about them.

Eventually the powers-that-be decided this bizarre apparition was a danger to the neighbourhood and it was condemned to be pulled down. An outcry went up across the States, but nothing could be done to stop these 'restorers of order'. The bulldozers and heavy equipment moved in to level the towers, but pull as they might they couldn't budge the well-constructed steel and concrete structures. Art and fantasy won to fight another day, and all the souls that need and love such expressions of joy felt the warmth of vindication.

Most of the mosaics I have featured in this chapter are chalky pastels but a very deep rich palette can be impressive as well. My London bathroom was completely tiled by the ceramicist Rupert Spira who also made my magnificent red and green striped basin.

I stitched a pair of needlepoint slippers in the bright colours of a Victorian mosaic pot found in an antique market to go with this scene. You will notice that I have used sharp contrasts and shadings of colours to give variety to the mosaic bits on my stitched slippers. They fit in wonderfully with the medieval tones of my bathroom (above). The toothbrush holder on the counter is Japanese *cloisonné* enamel and would make an excellent design for slippers, or a knitted or needlepoint cushion.

pots

Stunning porcelain pots have always been an important element in room decoration. They can be seen liberally sprinkled throughout most grand English houses, sitting in niches and on wall brackets, and serving as bases for lamps. In such settings they provide accents for glorious colour schemes. In other palatial Continental interiors, I have seen pots displayed so that they cover entire walls and become the overriding focus for the whole space – what a grand effect they make.

Because pots can have delicious shapes in silhouette they make gorgeous design motifs, either as simple flat depictions or as shaded renderings. Blue and white pots feature in Chinese wallpapers, on screens, in great tapestries and paintings. I have seen tapestry chairs with pots as a theme and carpets using them in borders. Deliciously, some Chinese blue and white pots are decorated all over with portraits of pots!

Carrying on this tradition of pot motifs, many contemporary design companies produce fabrics and wallpapers covered with blue and white pots. Neither the colour scheme nor the subject has lost its freshness or appeal.

Enthralled by them myself, I have collected pots of all sorts for years. I started with only shades of white pots which I painted in a large series of

LEFT: The *Cherry Blossom Cushion* and the *Flower Pot Chair* against my *Delft* fabric wall covering. OVERLEAF: A shock of Islamic blues in this neutral setting. The soft pastel curtains come from my still-life reflected in the mirror.

ABOVE: What a stunning decoration these simple bowls of fruit and pots of flowers make in the early eighteenth-century harem in Topkapi Palace, Istanbul.

white on white still-lifes. Then when I broke into oriental pattern-on-pattern in my painting and designing, I started collecting pots that were highly decorated in bold, delectable patterns. Lately I have been seduced by pure colours or washes of tone on pots that create intense pools of colour. A saturated apple green vase can spark off the colour in a series of duck-egg blue pots, or raspberry pink vessels next to turquoise pots can create a vivid glow.

Because I have collected pots for so long, it is small wonder that they crop up often in my work. I have knitted them into coats and sweaters, needlepointed them on to cushions, painted them in still-lifes, and used them as motifs on furnishing fabrics, wallpapers, mugs and tea cosies.

Having created a blue and white pots fabric for Designers Guild with bright yellow, green and red colourways, I was most struck by the quietest of the collection – a washy beige ground covered with graphite grey pots. Not only did this colourway have a lot of life in its understatement, but any colour looked wonderfully alive placed against it. Because it had these qualities I thought it would make a good base for my pots interior.

I have always loved fabrics and wallpapers that are predominantly sepia or shades of grey with a few details picked out in colour. There are, for example, designs where leaves and branches are perhaps depicted in monotone, while the occasional flower or butterfly shines out like a coloured jewel. My favourite window display, for Tiffany in New York, was a pile of dusty grey-brown leaves with a brilliant diamond brooch sitting on them. I saw that in the 1950s and have never forgotten it.

I had the same thrill of recognizing a unique sense of restrained colour when I visited Tage Andersen's shop in Copenhagen. This extraordinary artist works with flowers, fruits, leaves, burnished corroded metal and dried plant matter. His work is hauntingly beautiful. He is the only florist I have seen who can combine a pyramid of potatoes with pheasant feathers, shells and cabbages in an unforgettable autumnal arrangement.

Because so many of my colour statements are bright, not to say brash, it was stimulating to work from the restrained base of my beige and graphite pots fabric and to create a room that might appeal to a quieter nature. The fabric wall covering provides a neutral backdrop for other sharper colour accents.

My interior started with the fireplace surround made of old china shards and my off-white pot tiles. The beige and grey ground gives the mosaic a quiet glow. I painstakingly collected the mosaic ceramic pieces for the fireplace during walks across Hampstead Heath every morning.

As a bright accent for the pots room, I designed the needlepoint fire screen which was inspired by my collection of oriental blue and turquoise vases. When I put up the painting of my chock-a-block china dresser, it suddenly seemed to echo all the areas of colour in the room. The lacy pattern of my knitted *Pastel Pots Cushion* came from an

ABOVE: Nineteenth-century Chinese merchant's shop filled with porcelain. TOP: A wonderful display of oriental porcelain in Charlottenburg Palace, Berlin.

Indian fretwork shelf. I chose bright pastel pots to softly shine against the beige shades of the ground.

The hydrangeas with their mysterious pinks and greeny-blues were a finishing touch that added a little smouldering richness to the room.

Cherry Blossom Cushion

Size of cushion

The finished cushion measures 54cm (21½in) wide by 53cm (21¼in) tall.

Materials

- ROWAN *Lightweight DK* (25g/1oz hanks) in the following 11 colours:

A	Sienna	86	5 hanks
B	Light coral	79	1 hank
C	Ecru	614	1 hank
D	Light brown	59	1 hank
E	Light blue	48	1 hank
F	Mustard	5	1 hank
G	Pale purple	120	1 hank
H	Light green	416	1 hank
J	Off white	1	1 hank
L	Pale lilac	109	3 hanks
M	Dark blue	53	3 hanks

- One pair 3¾mm (US size 5) knitting needles
- Small piece of scrap fabric for backing the knitting
- 70cm (¾yd) of 90cm (36in) wide fabric for cushion cover back and matching sewing thread
- 48cm (19in) zipper
- Cushion pad (pillow form) same size as finished cover or slightly larger

Knitting stitch gauge

28 sts and 30 rows to 10cm (4in) measured over colourwork pattern using 3¾mm (US size 5) knitting needles.

Special notes

When working the colourwork pattern, use the intarsia method for working the background mosaic shapes, using a separate length of yarn for each mosaic shape and linking one colour to the next by twisting them around each other on WS where they meet to avoid holes. Use the Fair Isle technique for the mosaic outline colour (yarn A) in the background, carrying yarn A when not in use loosely across the WS of the background and weaving it in every 3 or 4 sts to avoid

ABOVE: Never settling for an easy life, I decided to paint all of my favourite pots in one go!

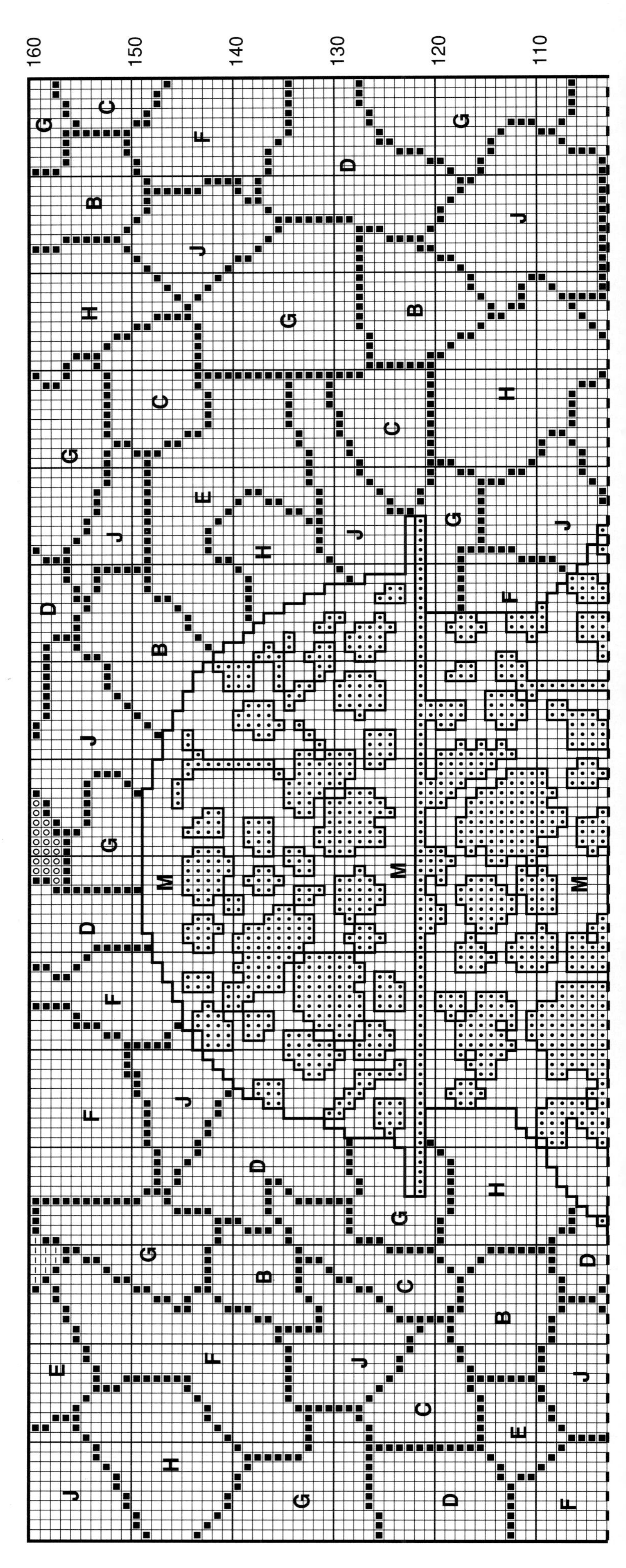

long loose ends. Use the Fair Isle technique for the pot, but link pot to background with intarsia technique.
Read chart from right to left for k rows and from left to right for p rows.

Charted pot and mosaic design

Using yarn A, cast on 150 sts.
Beg with a k row, work 160 rows in st st following chart for colourwork pattern.
Using yarn A, cast (bind) off loosely.

Finishing the cushion cover

Press lightly on WS with a damp cloth and a warm iron.
Cut a piece of scrap fabric the same size as the knitting plus a 1.5cm (½in) seam allowance all around the edge.
With the wrong sides facing each other, pin the knitting to the centre of this piece of fabric. Then sew the two layers together, stitching close to the edge of the knitting.
Sew the zipper between two pieces of fabric for the cushion cover back and join the front and back of the cover as instructed on page 152, catching the edge of the knitting into the seam.

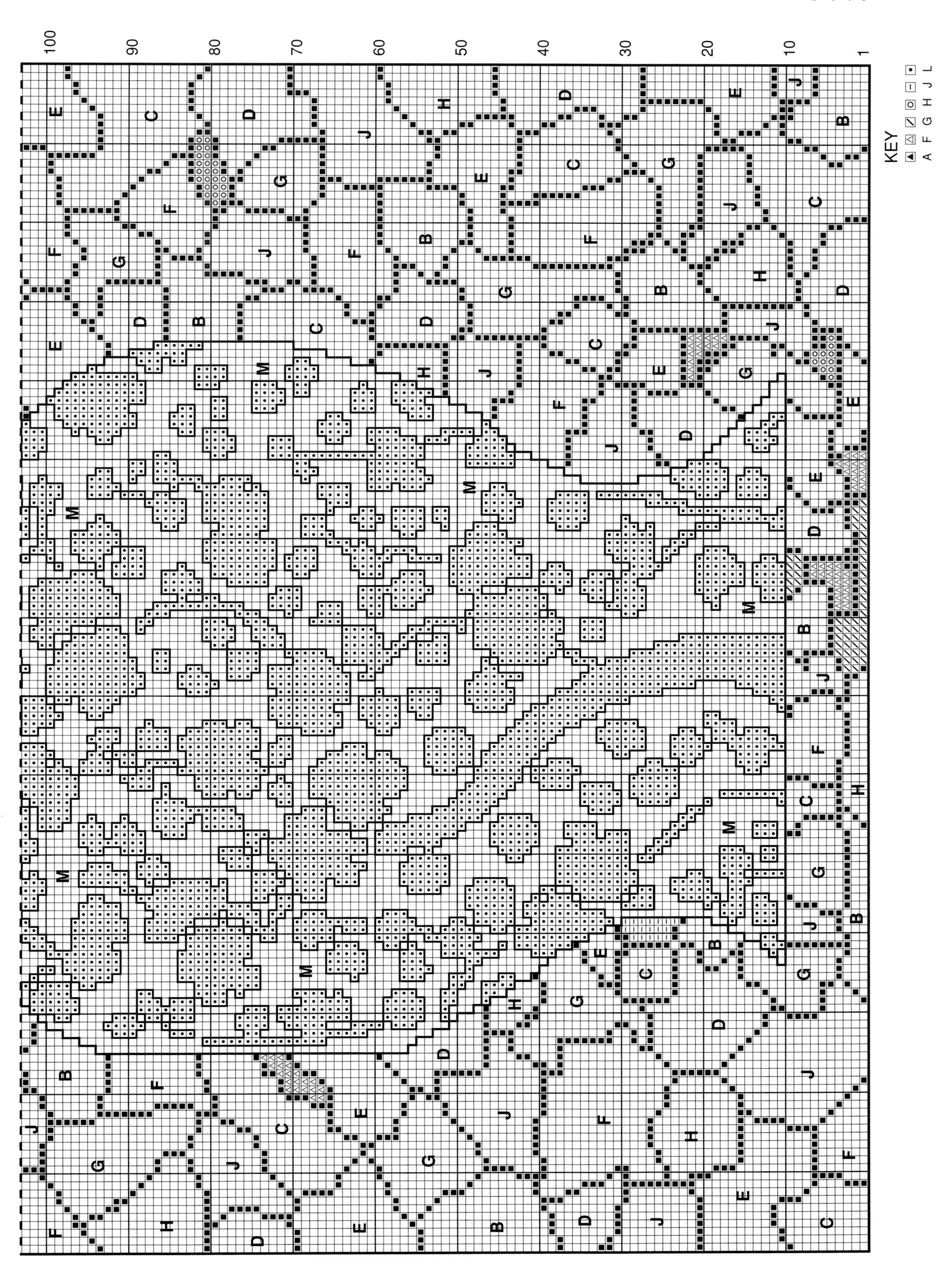
KEY
A F G H J L

ABOVE: Thumbing through a book on India led me to the lacy design on the *Pastel Pots Cushion*. The fireplace is made of my pot tiles and ceramic shards.

Pastel Pots Cushion

Size of cushion

The finished cushion measures 50cm (20in) wide by 50cm (20in) tall.

Materials

- ROWAN *Lightweight DK* (25g/1oz hanks) in the following 17 colours:

A	Off white	1	4 hanks
B	Light brown	613	4 hanks
C	Bright green	431	small amount
D	Mid blue	51	small amount
E	Sea green	89	small amount
F	Tangerine	16	small amount
G	Lime	33	small amount
H	Coral	22	small amount
J	Light blue	123	small amount
L	Lilac	128	small amount
M	Mustard	8	small amount
N	Gold	72	small amount
O	Pale coral	20	small amount

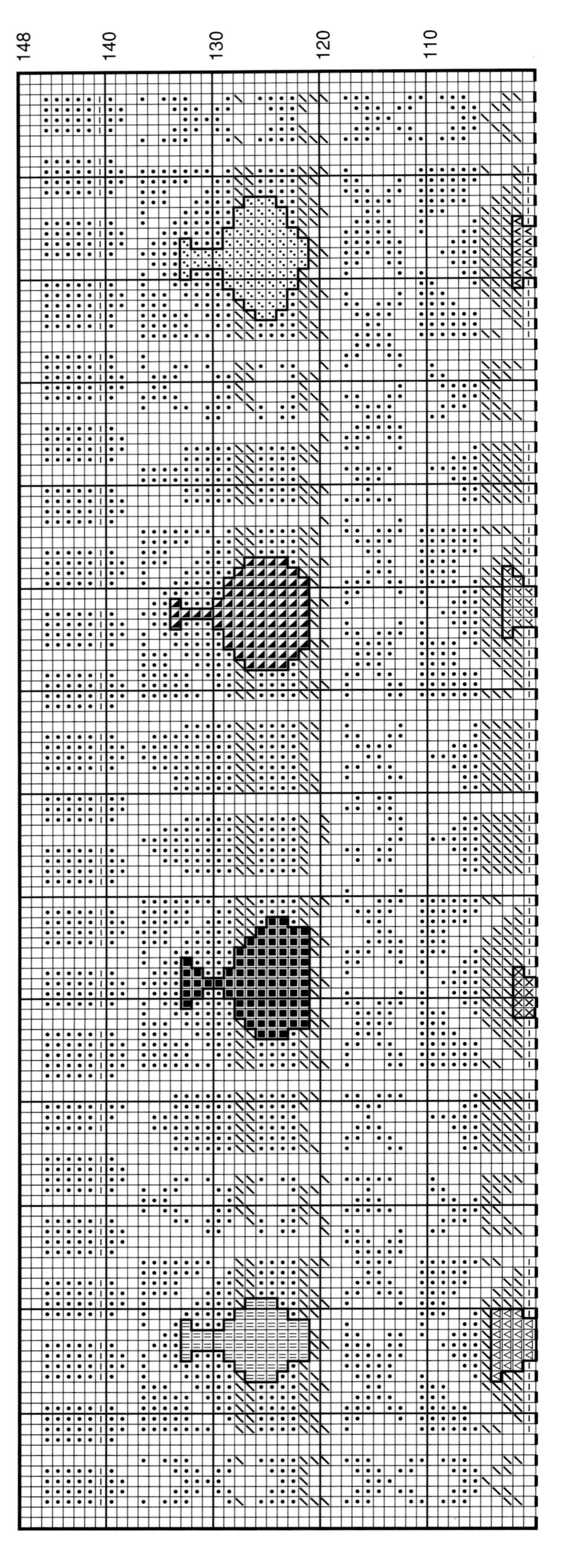

100 90 80 70 60 50 40 30 20 10 1
KEY
A B C D E F G H J L M N O Q R S T U V

Q	Yellow	116	small amount
R	Light pink	68	small amount
S	Pale sea green	416	small amount
T	Grass green	36	small amount

• ROWAN *Donegal Lambswool Tweed* (25g/1oz hanks) in the following colour:

U	Rye	474	2 hanks

• ROWAN *Kid Silk* (25g/1oz balls) in the following colour:

V	Turnip	997	1 ball

• One pair of 3¾mm (US size 5) knitting needles
• Small piece of scrap fabric for backing the knitting
• 70cm (¾yd) of 90cm (36in) wide fabric for cushion cover back and matching sewing thread
• 45cm (18in) zipper
• Cushion pad (pillow form) same size as finished cover or slightly larger

Knitting stitch gauge

28 sts and 30 rows to 10cm (4in) measured over colourwork pattern using 3¾mm (US size 5) knitting needles.

Special notes

All 15 colours used for the small pots require only a small amount of yarn. Instead of buying a whole hank of each of these colours, you could used leftover yarns in similar shades.
When working the colourwork pattern, use a mixture of the Fair Isle and intarsia techniques. Use the intarsia method for working the individual pots, using a separate length of yarn for each pot and linking the pot colour to the background colour by twisting the colours around each other on WS where they meet to avoid holes.
Use the Fair Isle method for working the background in yarn A and yarn B (or yarns U and V), carrying the colour not in use loosely across the WS and weaving it in every 3 or 4 sts to avoid long loose ends at the back of the work.
Read chart from right to left for k (RS odd-numbered) rows and from left to right for p (WS even-numbered) rows.

Charted pots design

Using yarn B, cast on 141 sts.
P one row.
Beg with a k row, work 148 rows in st st following chart for colourwork pattern (see special notes for colourwork instructions), so ending with a p row.
Using yarn B, k one row.
Using yarn B, cast (bind) off loosely purlwise.

Finishing the cushion cover

Press lightly on WS with a damp cloth and a warm iron.
Cut a piece of scrap fabric the same size as the knitting plus a 1.5cm (½in) seam allowance all around the edge.
Complete this cushion cover as for *Cherry Blossom Cushion* on page 94.

Blue Jars Fire Screen

Size of fire screen

The finished needlepoint measures 41cm (16¼in) wide by 54cm (21¼in) tall.
Note: This needlepoint could also be made into a cushion cover. See another needlepoint cover for materials needed.

Materials

• 10-mesh single- or double-thread canvas 56cm (22in) by 69cm (27in)
• ANCHOR wool tapestry yarn in the 17 colours listed below
• Size 18 tapestry needle
• Wooden fire screen frame

Yarn colours and amounts

You will need Anchor wool tapestry yarn (10m/11yd skeins) in the following 17 colours and approximate amounts:

A	Deep peacock green	8924	3 skeins
B	Mid aqua	8938	4 skeins
C	Light peacock green	8916	4 skeins
D	Pale jade	8962	3 skeins

RIGHT: The *Blue Jars Fire Screen* is a portrait of my Islamic pot collection. The many rich shades of blue and lavender on the needlepoint really sing, and the chartreuse gives an added kick.

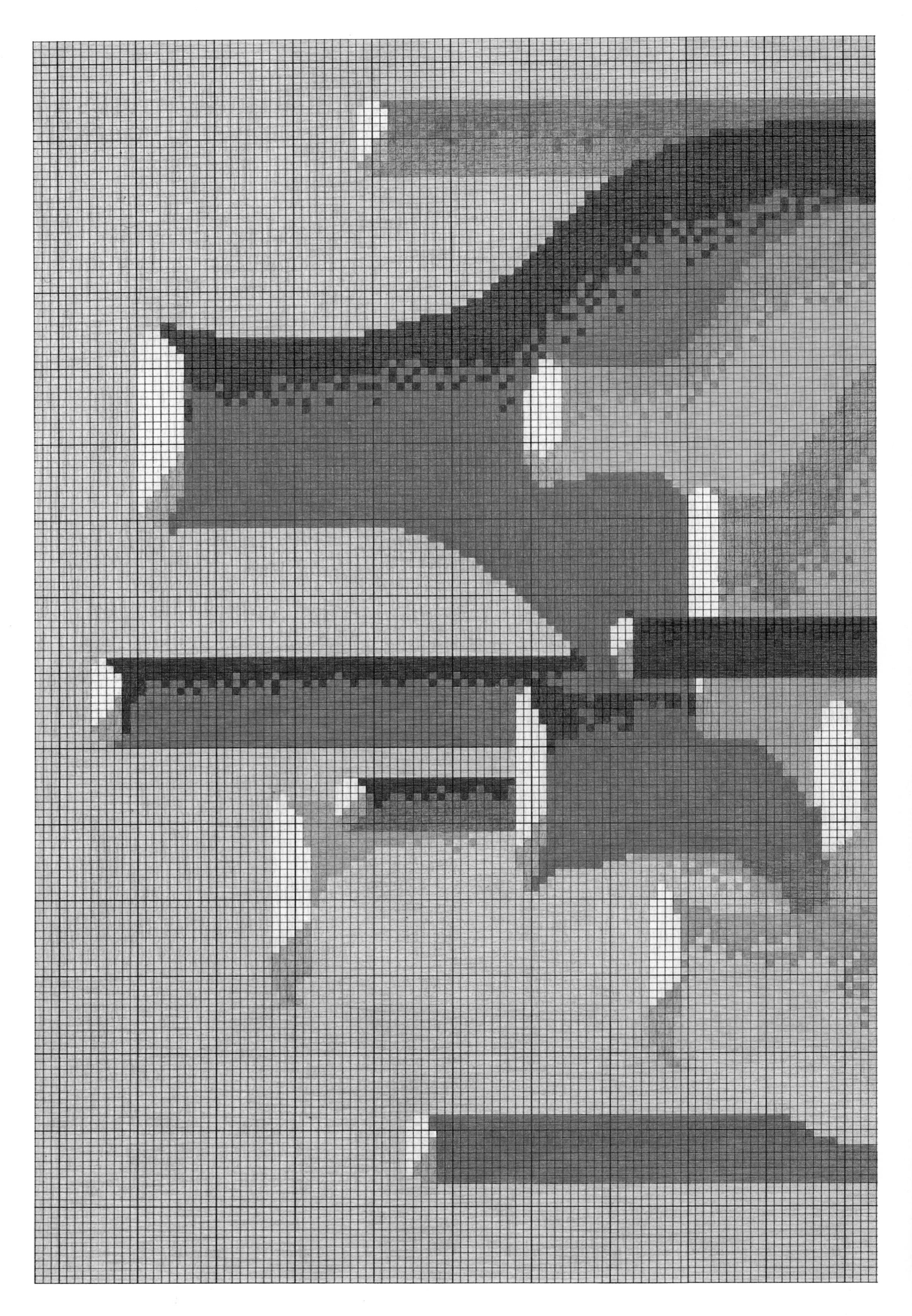

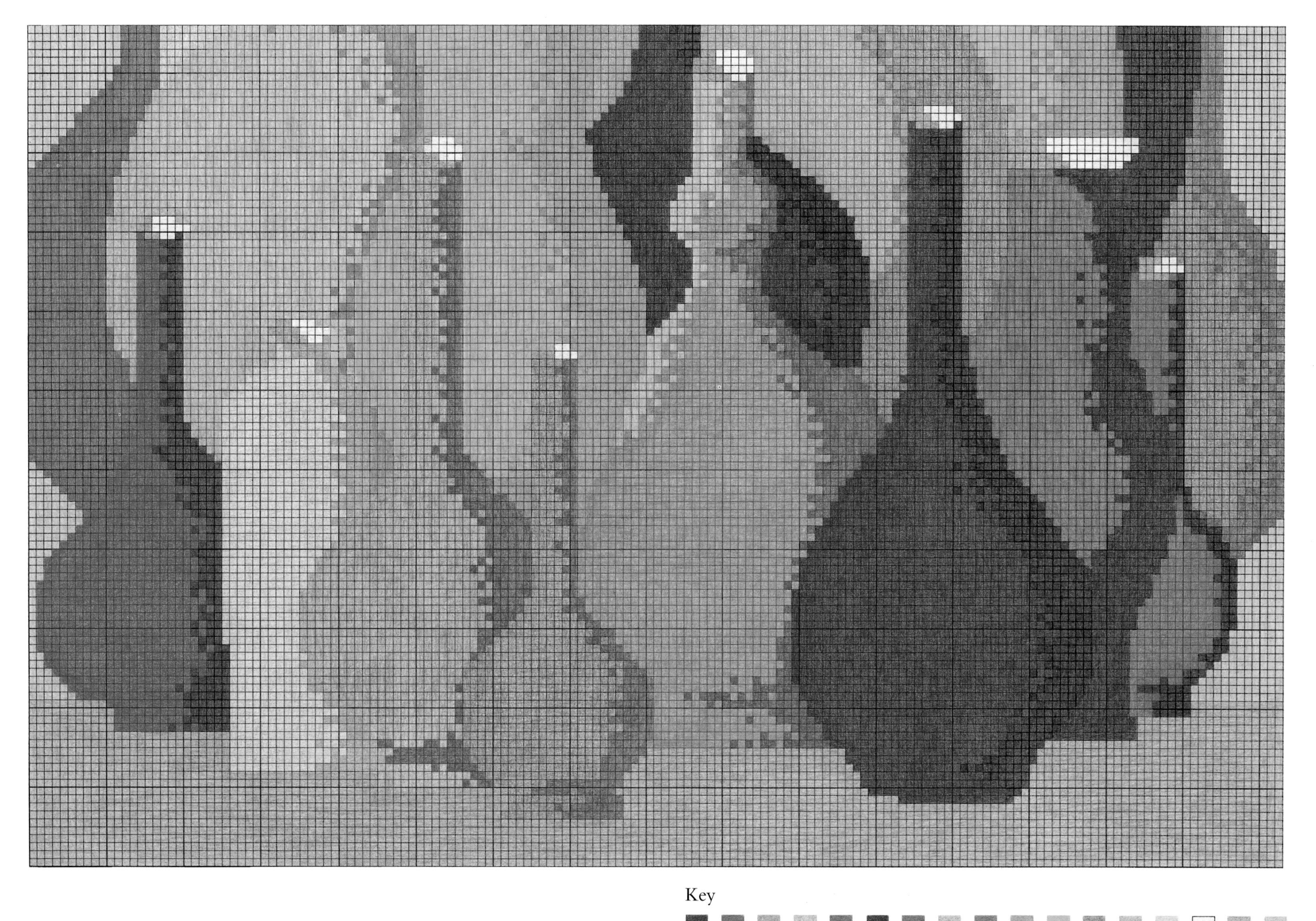
Key
A B C D E F G H I J K L M N O P Q

ABOVE: I decorated these pot tiles specially for this Rye kitchen. TOP: A fabulous use of plates in a Transylvanian dining room. RIGHT: The cool green pots bathroom with the *Pots Collage Border*.

E	Turquoise	8808	3 skeins
F	Dark cornflower blue	8690	4 skeins
G	Mid cornflower blue	8688	2 skeins
H	Light cornflower blue	8686	2 skeins
I	Mid apple green	9102	2 skeins
J	Light lime	9274	2 skeins
K	Pale parrot green	9152	3 skeins
L	Mid lilac	8588	3 skeins
M	Light purple	8524	2 skeins
N	Pale purple	8522	3 skeins
O	Off white	8006	2 skeins
P	Mid gobelin green	8876	4 skeins
Q	Pale olive green	9172	11 skeins

Working the embroidery

The chart is 163 stitches wide and 213 stitches tall. Begin by marking the outline of the design on to your canvas and, if desired, dividing it into tens just like the charted design. Make a paper template of the design outline and set aside to use later as a guide for blocking.

Following the chart, work the embroidery in tent stitch, using one strand of Anchor wool tapestry yarn (see page 150 for tent stitch techniques). Work the pots first, leaving the background at the top (pale olive green, shade no. 9172) and the background at the bottom (mid gobelin green, shade no. 8876) until last.

Finishing the fire screen

After the embroidery has been completed, block the canvas, using the paper template as your guide (see page 152 for detailed blocking instructions).

Do not trim the canvas edges until the needlepoint has been mounted on the fire screen base.

My starting point for the pots bathroom was some blue and white pot wallpaper that I created for Designers Guild. When designing it, I had first painted it with a mulberry stippled ground and a bright yellow colourway, but Tricia Guild suggested this cool mint ground. I must say, it produces a wonderfully soft and peaceful atmosphere that turns the bathroom into a sanctuary.

My wallpaper base inspired the jug border that runs around the top of the walls. I cut a thin cardboard template in the shape of a jug and used it to trace pots onto different dusty blue Designers Guild wallpapers. Every other pot in the border is darker, which creates a nice rhythm. The idea for these pots came from those classic old English jugs with all-over patterns that I call 'wallpaper jugs'.

Antique Victorian florid blue and white basins and toilets are lovely. I am glad to see some firms bringing back a bit of decoration to the plain white basin. The basin in my bathroom interior looks so good with the

wallpaper and painted ceramic pots that sit next to it. The enamelled pink taps are probably 1930s and were found at the Brighton flea market. That dusty pink is in perfect harmony with the mint green.

To go with this soft green interior, I designed the rag rug of blue and white pots. Making the rug was an exercise in finding as many shades of greens, pale blues, and turquoises as possible for the background. If you want the pots on the *Pots Rag Rug* to read more clearly, do them in dark blues and crisp white with no shadows.

For an exotic finishing touch for the room, I added the little carved Indonesian shelves which I found in a Balinese shop. Their faded paintwork complemented my old blue mirror. This peeling frame and corroded mirror appealed to me long before these distressed surfaces became fashionable.

ABOVE: This carved Balinese wall shelf looks so at home on the cool green *Pots* wallpaper designed for Designers Guild. RIGHT: Multicoloured rags create a soft focus on the *Pots Rag Rug*.

Pots Rag Rug

Size of rag rug

The finished rag rug measures 75cm (30in) wide by 120cm (48in) long.

Materials

- Piece of loose-weave hessian (burlap) at least 91cm (36in) by 134cm (53in)
- Variety of scrap fabrics for strips (see *Choosing the colours* below)
- Large rug hook
- 4.3m (4¾yd) of 6cm (2½in) wide twilled carpet binding tape (optional)
- Strong thread for hemming

Choosing the colours

You will need scrap fabrics in a variety of colours and in a range of tones. Study the photograph of the rug for an idea of the types of colours to choose. Then look for scraps to fit into this scheme or to fit into your own original palette. (See page 147 for information on fabrics suitable for rag rugs.)

Transferring the design

Using a dressmaker's marking pen, mark the outer outline of the rug on to the right side of the hessian (burlap). The dimensions of the outer outline are given on the left under *Size of rag rug* and are shown on the rug design diagram. Allow at least 8cm (3in) of extra fabric all around the edge.

Following the rug diagram, transfer the rug design on to the right side of the fabric as instructed on page 148.

Preparing the rag strips

Cut some of the fabric scraps into strips 1.5cm (½in) to 2.5cm (1in) wide, depending on the thickness of the fabric. Cut only enough strips to provide a variety of tones and shades for working the first pot. Cut the remaining scraps only when you need them as the work progresses.

A detailed explanation of how to cut strips for rag rugs is given on page 148.

Hooking the rug

Before starting to hook the rug, read the hooking instructions on page 149.

Note: Each square on the grid represents 10cm (4in).

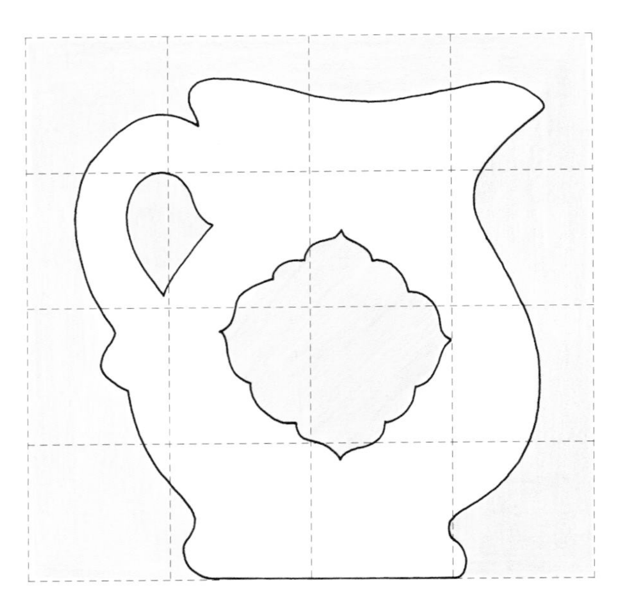

LEFT: A detail of the pots bathroom showing the 1930s pink enamel taps bought in a flea market.
ABOVE: The *Pots Collage Border* motif.

Then begin the rug by working the pots at the centre of the design, using rag strips of the desired colour. (As a guideline, the rug diagram indicates some of the colours used on the original *Pots Rag Rug*.)

After completing the pots, work the triangles at the four corners of the rug. Then work the outer border in diagonal stripes, leaving the background until last.

Finishing the rug

After the hooking has been completed, bind the edges of the hessian (burlap) if desired, then turn back the edges and work the hem, mitring the corners. Turn to page 149 for finishing instructions.

Pots Collage Border

Materials

- Plain-coloured wallpaper for collage base
- Wallpaper paste
- Selection of wallpaper scraps

Preparing the collage cutouts

Enlarge the pot design on to a piece of thin cardboard. Begin by drawing the outer outline of the grid which is 20cm (8in) by 20cm (8in). Then draw the 5cm (2in) squares of the grid. Following the diagram shown above, copy the pot and the central motif on to the grid. Trace the central motif and transfer it on to another piece of thin cardboard. Cut out both the pot and the central motif.

Using the cardboard cutouts as templates, trace around the shapes on a variety of wallpaper scraps until you have the required number of pots and the same number of contrasting central motifs.

Applying the collage cutouts

Using the wallpaper paste, apply the strip of plain coloured wallpaper in the desired position on the wall.

Apply the cut-out pots along the plain wallpaper border. Then apply the contrasting central motifs on top of the pots. (See page 153 for more detailed instructions for collage techniques.)

leaves

Individual leaves with their many shapes and variations of greens are elegant even before autumn when they go mad with shades of gold, red and pink. Though each spring seems even better than the previous one, there is definitely a special place in my heart for autumn. It comes after a long, wonderful summer when you feel lazy and spoiled by warmth and light. Gradually you sense the sharpness in the air and the shock of a few leaves turning red or mellow gold like bright parrot feathers. Then quite suddenly a sheer mass of yellow fills the crisp, clear, deliciously cold air. Every year I have to fight back the tendency to carry armloads of bright leaves home. Simply walking in the woods is like going to exhibitions of the most gorgeous paintings.

So many artists and decorators have used leaves with much the same passion as I have. I think of the great canopy of a banana tree that crowns the Royal Pavilion banqueting hall in Brighton. Its larger than life leaves fill a domed ceiling to dramatic effect. This oriental pavilion with its unique colour scheme was one of my most powerful first impressions on arriving in England thirty years ago.

LEFT: Celebrating fruits and leafy vegetables, my *Cabbage and Melon* needlepoint chair sits comfortably against the garden mural. OVERLEAF: I wanted this leaf dining room to be like a clearing in the woods.

Another image that haunts me is an Italian room with a fresco of a rustic arbour covered in leaves. The thing that stays forever in my brain is how secure and happy I felt in this leafy room. The rough lattice of brown sticks with leaves on the fresco was such a simple idea but obviously haunting! I later painted a mural in a Cotswolds house of an overgrown jungle theme and, remembering the Italian rustic room, I painted a border of sticks all around it.

My leaf room grew directly from the amazing hand-blocked wallpaper panels from Alexander Beauchamp. The founder, Karen Beauchamp, contacted me when she heard I was doing this book and told me she was resurrecting old Sanderson's landscape mural papers. The repeat of the Kew Gardens scene was made up of twelve panels and it came in three colourways. Since I wanted the dense tapestry effect and one repeat of the mural was only a few feet high, I decided to collage together the different colourways. I was delighted with the end result, even though it took days of cutting and pasting.

When applying the wallpaper, we began with the softest grey colourway at the top. Then starting from a different point in the

ABOVE: Late eighteenth-century decoration painted by Johann Bergl in the Schönbrunn Palace, Vienna. TOP: Early nineteenth-century wallpaper by Mongin. TOP LEFT: These *Leaf Slippers* are available as a kit.

series, we proceeded with the next layer in the sepia colourway, carefully cutting away any trace of 'sky'. Lastly, we cut and pasted the deeply toned autumn colourway. A densely detailed oriental carpet in soft golds, oranges and olives and the crumbling old gilt mirror completed the 'shell' of my room.

A gorgeous reproduction tapestry brought the leafy theme across to the table. The stunning nineteenth-century English majolica ware provides spontaneous washes of deep toned glazes that create the perfect highlight for the room. A friend who makes props for television made me the extravagant painted cloth cabbages using a football as a base!

I tried to keep in mind the greys, sepias, and deep rather serious autumn tones of the wallpaper when designing my cushions and the knitted *Leaf Throw*. I occasionally lifted the palette to create high notes but always used as many of the actual colours in the paper as possible. The knitted *Madiera Cushion,* inspired by a pot resplendent with fruit and leaves, stays nicely within this scheme.

The duck-egg blue of the needlepoint *Melon Chair* sparks off the many shades of green, yellow and peach, keeping the all-over effect high and light-hearted. This chair would look gorgeous in a yellow or pale green room, but it sits happily in here with its mossy leaves blending with the leafy surroundings.

I was once struck by a handsome dining room of dark trees in the Merchant-Ivory film *The Europeans*. The grand presence of a group of trees made a very liveable backdrop for a room. When designing this interior, perhaps I was recalling those little clearings in the woods where you feel you have stumbled into a magic place – an inner chamber with walls of foliage.

ABOVE: What a grand impact this banana tree makes on the ceiling in the Royal Pavilion in Brighton, Sussex.

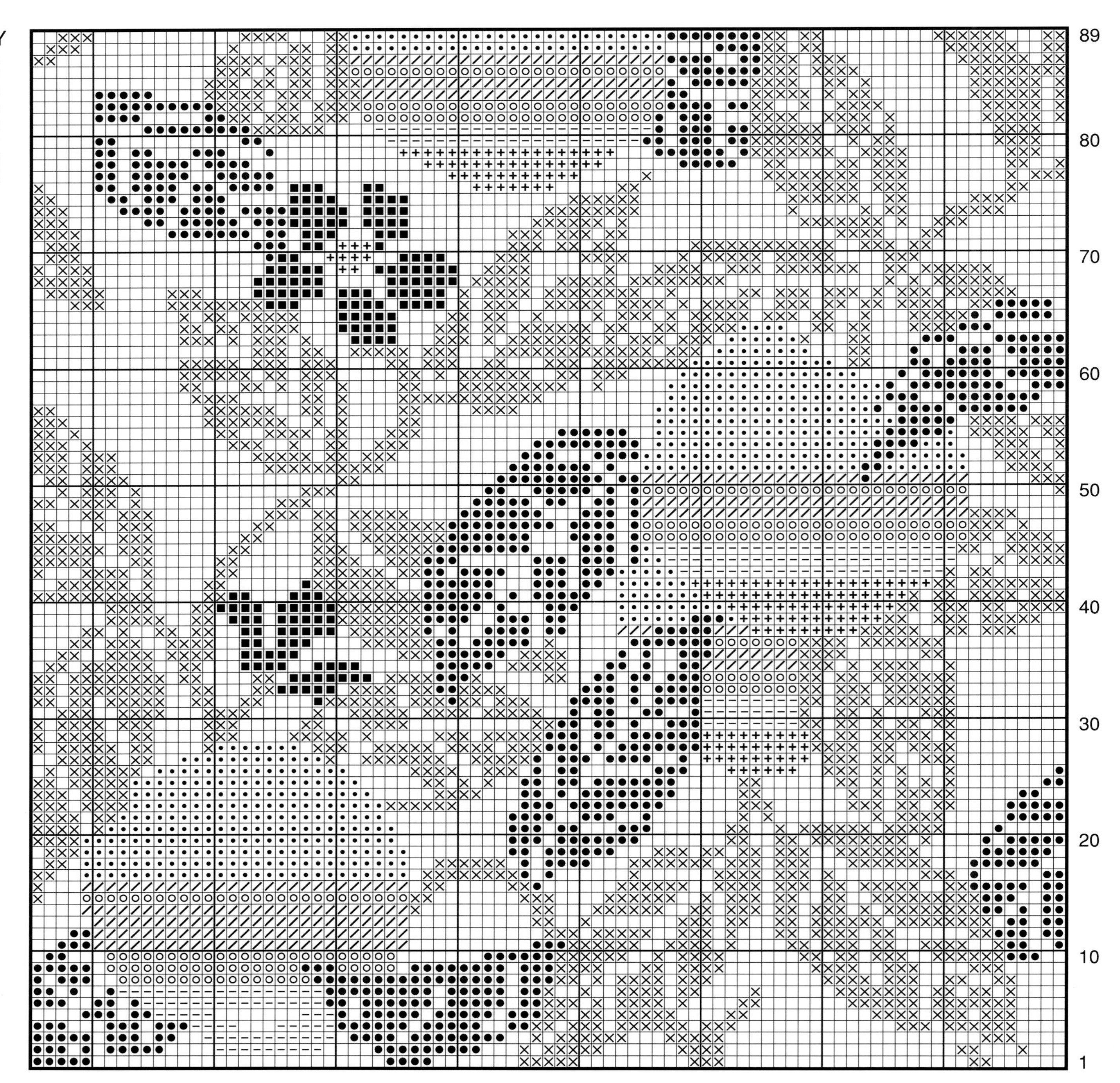

Madeira Cushion

Size of cushion

The finished cushion measures 43cm (17in) wide by 41cm (16in) tall.

Materials

- PATERNA/YAN *Persian Yarn* in the following 9 colours:

A	Deep plum	320	360m (393yd)
B	Pearl grey	212	280m (306yd)
C	Hunter green	612	70m (77yd)
D	Honey gold	732	28m (31yd)
E	Copper	862	28m (31yd)
F	Rusty rose	930	28m (31yd)
G	American beauty	900	40m (44yd)
H	Autumn yellow	726	20m (22yd)
J	Bittersweet	835	20m (22yd)

- One pair of 5mm (US size 8) knitting needles
- Small piece of scrap fabric for backing the knitting
- 70cm (¾yd) of 90cm (36in) wide fabric for cushion cover back and matching sewing thread
- 38cm (15in) zipper

ABOVE: The *Madeira Cushion* (left) standing next to its ceramic pot inspiration, and the *Tapestry Leaf Cushion* (right).

- Cushion pad (pillow form) same size as finished cover or slightly larger

Knitting stitch gauge

19 sts and 24 rows to 10cm (4in) measured over st st using all three strands of the Persian Yarn and 5mm (US size 8) knitting needles.
20 sts and 22 rows to 10cm (4in) measured over colourwork pattern using 5mm (US size 8) knitting needles.

Special notes

When working the colourwork pattern, use a mixture of the Fair Isle and intarsia techniques. Use the Fair Isle method for working the background in yarn A and the leaves in yarn B (or in yarn C), carrying the colour not in use loosely across the WS of the areas worked in A and B (or C) and weaving it in every 3 or 4 sts to avoid long loose ends. For the flowers and fruit, use the intarsia method, using a separate length of yarn for each area of colour and linking one colour to the next by twisting them around each other on WS where they meet to avoid holes. Do not carry any other yarn across the WS of the fruits (in yarns D, E, F, G and H).
Read chart from right to left for k (RS odd-numbered) rows and from left to right for p (WS even-numbered) rows.
All three strands of the Persian Yarn are used together throughout. See page 157 for calculating number of skeins or hanks required. When purchasing Persian Yarn for knitting, be sure to purchase continuous skeins/hanks instead of lengths already precut for needlepoint.

Charted leaf and fruit design

Using yarn A, cast on 85 sts. Then beg with a k row, work 89 rows in st st following chart for colourwork pattern (see special notes), so ending with a k row.
Using A, cast (bind) off loosely.

Finishing the cushion cover

Press knitting lightly on WS with a damp cloth and a warm iron.

Cut a piece of scrap fabric the same size as the knitting plus a 1.5cm (1/2in) seam allowance all around the edge.
With the wrong sides facing each other, pin the knitting to the centre of this piece of fabric. Then sew the two layers together, working small running stitches very close to the edge of the knitting.
Using the zipper foot on your sewing machine or stitching by hand, sew the zipper between two pieces of fabric for the cushion cover back and join the front and back of the cover as instructed on page 152, catching the edge of the knitting into the seam as it is joined.

Cabbage Leaf Rag Rug

Size of rag rug

The finished rag rug measures 120cm (48in) wide by 90cm (36in) tall.

Materials

- Piece of loose-weave hessian (burlap) at least 136cm (54in) by 106cm (42in)
- Variety of scrap fabrics for strips (see *Choosing the colours* below)
- Large rug hook
- 4.5m (5yd) of 6cm (2 1/2in) wide twilled carpet binding tape (optional)
- Strong thread for hemming

Choosing the colours

You will need scrap fabrics in a variety of colours and in a range of tones. Study the photograph of the rug for an idea of the types of colours to choose. Then look for scraps to fit into this scheme or to fit into your own original palette. (See page 147 for information on types of fabrics suitable for rag rugs.)

BELOW: It was a challenge to shade the voluptuous cabbage on the rag rug without dyeing the rags.

Transferring the design

Using a dressmaker's marking pen, mark the outer outline of the rug on to the right side of the hessian (burlap). The dimensions of the outer outline are given on page 116 under *Size of rag rug* and are shown on the rug design diagram. Allow at least 8cm (3in) of extra fabric all around the edge.

Following the rag rug diagram shown below, transfer the rug design on to the right side of the fabric as instructed in the rag rug techniques section on page 148.

Preparing the rag strips

Cut some of the fabric scraps into strips 1.5cm (½in) to 2.5cm (1in) wide, depending on the thickness of the fabric. Cut only enough strips to provide a variety of tones and shades for working a small section of the cabbage. Cut the remaining scraps only when you need them as the work progresses.

A detailed explanation of how to cut strips for rag rugs is given on page 148.

Hooking the rug

Before starting to hook the rug, read the hooking instructions on page 149. Then begin the rug by working the cabbage, using rag strips of the desired colour. (As a guideline, the rug diagram indicates some of the colours used on the original *Cabbage Rag Rug*. Follow the photograph for further guidance.)

After completing the cabbage, work the leaves around the cabbage, leaving the background until last.

Finishing the rug

After the hooking has been completed, bind the edges of the hessian (burlap) if desired, then turn back the edges and work the hem, mitring the corners. Turn to page 149 for finishing instructions.

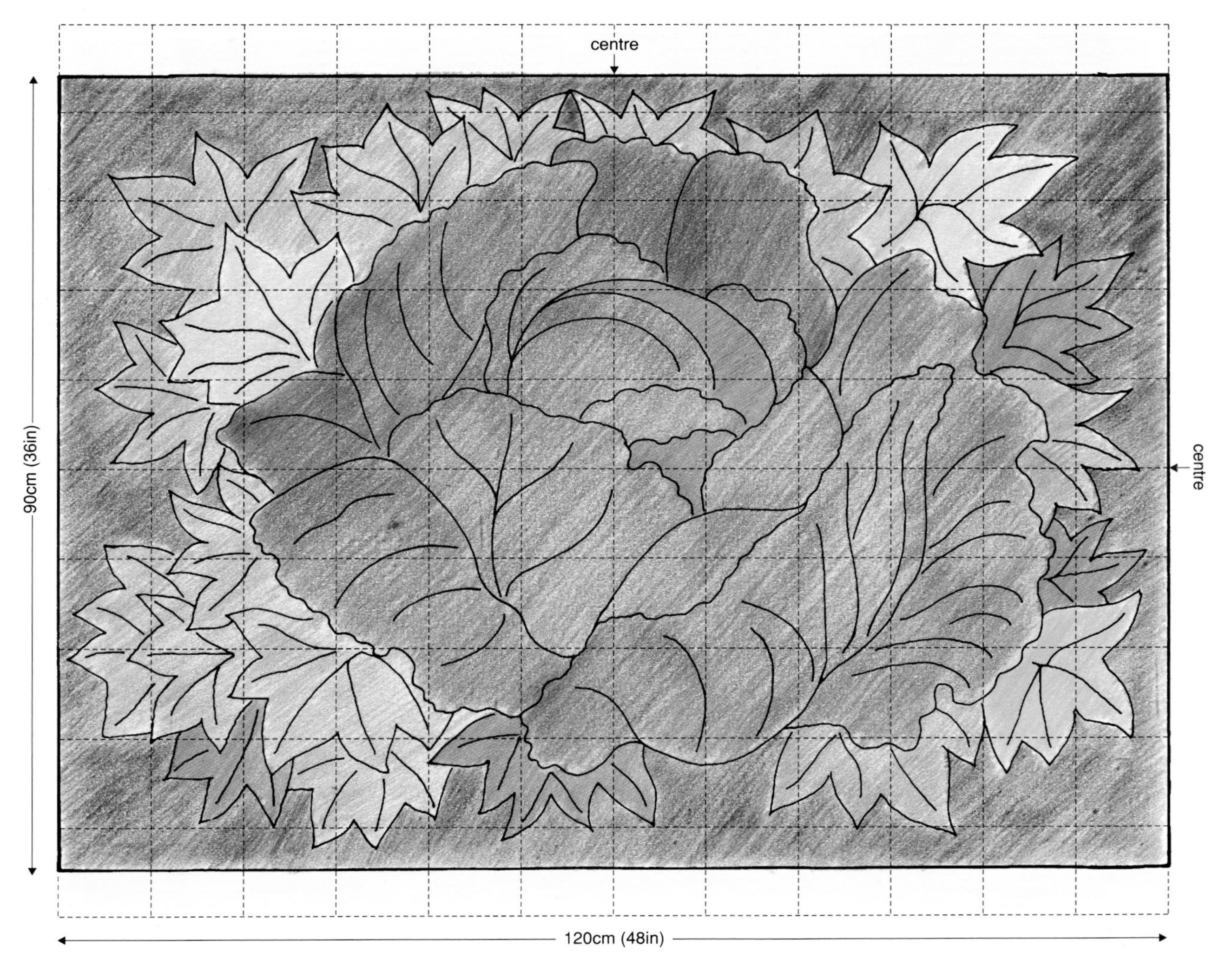

Note: Each square on the grid represents 10cm (4in).

Overlapping Leaf Cushion

Size of cushion

The finished cushion measures 42cm (16½in) wide by 42cm (16½in) tall.

Materials

- 10-mesh single- or double-thread canvas 56cm (22in) square
- ANCHOR wool tapestry yarn in the 14 colours listed on page 120
- Size 18 tapestry needle
- 70cm (¾yd) of 90cm (36in) wide backing fabric and matching sewing thread
- 1.8m (2yd) of piping (filling) cord or ready-made cord (optional)
- 35cm (14in) zipper
- Cushion pad (pillow form) same size as finished cover or slightly larger

Yarn colours and amounts

You will need Anchor wool tapestry yarn (10m/11yd skeins) in the following 14 colours and approximate amounts:

ABOVE: Frosty winter leaves inspired the design for the *Overlapping Leaf Cushion*. I'm really happy with way the cushion harmonizes with the old French metal chair and the antique tones of the wallpaper.

Key

- A
- B
- C
- D
- E
- F
- G
- H
- I
- J
- K
- L
- M
- N

A	Deep ocean blue	8838	7 skeins
B	Mid sea green	8900	2 skeins
C	Dark forest green	9022	3 skeins
D	Mid forest green	9020	3 skeins
E	Light laurel green	9002	4 skeins
F	Pale spruce green	9074	2 skeins
G	Dark brown olive	9310	2 skeins
H	Mid moss green	9214	4 skeins
I	Bright leaf green	9194	3 skeins
J	Mid mink	9680	4 skeins
K	Light mink	9676	5 skeins
L	Pale cloud grey	8706	3 skeins
M	Pale khaki	9324	3 skeins
N	Pale snuff brown	9484	4 skeins

Working the embroidery

The chart is 164 stitches wide and 165 stitches tall. Begin by marking the outline of the design on to your canvas and, if desired, dividing it into tens just like the charted design. Make a paper template of the design outline and set aside to use later as a guide for blocking.

Following the chart on pages 118 and 119, work the embroidery in tent stitch, using one strand of Anchor wool tapestry yarn (see page 150 for instructions for various tent stitch techniques). Note that the leaf outlines are worked in three pale colours (pale cloud grey, pale khaki and pale snuff brown, shade nos. 8706, 9324 and 9484).

Finishing the cushion cover

After the embroidery has been completed, block the needlepoint canvas, using the paper template as your guide (see page 152 for blocking instructions).

Trim the canvas edges, leaving a seam allowance of 2cm (3/4in).

Sew the zipper between two pieces of fabric for the cushion cover back as instructed on page 152.

If desired, cover the piping (filling) cord and pin to the needlepoint. Then join the front and back of the cover as described on page 152. If you are using a ready-made cord as a trimming, sew it to the completed cover, tucking the ends into a small opening in the seam.

Leaf Throw

Size of throw

The finished throw measures 159cm (63¼in) wide by 157cm (62¾in) long. The knitted centre square measures approximately 106cm (42¼in) by 104cm (41¾in) excluding the border. The border measures approximately 26.5cm (10½in) deep.

Materials

- ROWAN *Donegal Lambswool Tweed* (25g/1oz hanks) in the following 16 colours:

A	Dolphin	478	29 hanks
B	Oatmeal	469	4 hanks
C	Cinnamon	479	4 hanks
D	Nutmeg	470	4 hanks
E	Rye	474	4 hanks
F	Leaf	481	3 hanks
G	Tarragon	477	2 hanks
H	Dried rose	462	2 hanks
J	Roseberry	480	3 hanks
L	Mulberry	459	2 hanks
M	Blue mist	476	3 hanks
N	Eau de nil	458	1 hank
O	Chilli	464	2 hanks
Q	Dragonfly	488	2 hanks
R	Sedge	471	1 hank
S	Bramble	484	1 hank
T	Juniper	482	1 hank
U	Teal	456	1 hank

- Long circular 6mm (US size 10) knitting needle
- 4.50mm (US size G) crochet hook

Knitting stitch gauge

17 sts and 21 rows to 10cm (4in) measured over colourwork pattern using yarn doubled and 6mm (US size 10) knitting needles.

Special notes

The yarn is used double throughout. The yarns are used in various combinations: for example, AA means 2 strands of yarn A used together, CD means one strand of C and

RIGHT: I used two strands of Rowan's tweed yarn together when knitting the *Leaf Throw*. This enabled me to mix colours, creating enough tones for smooth shading transitions.

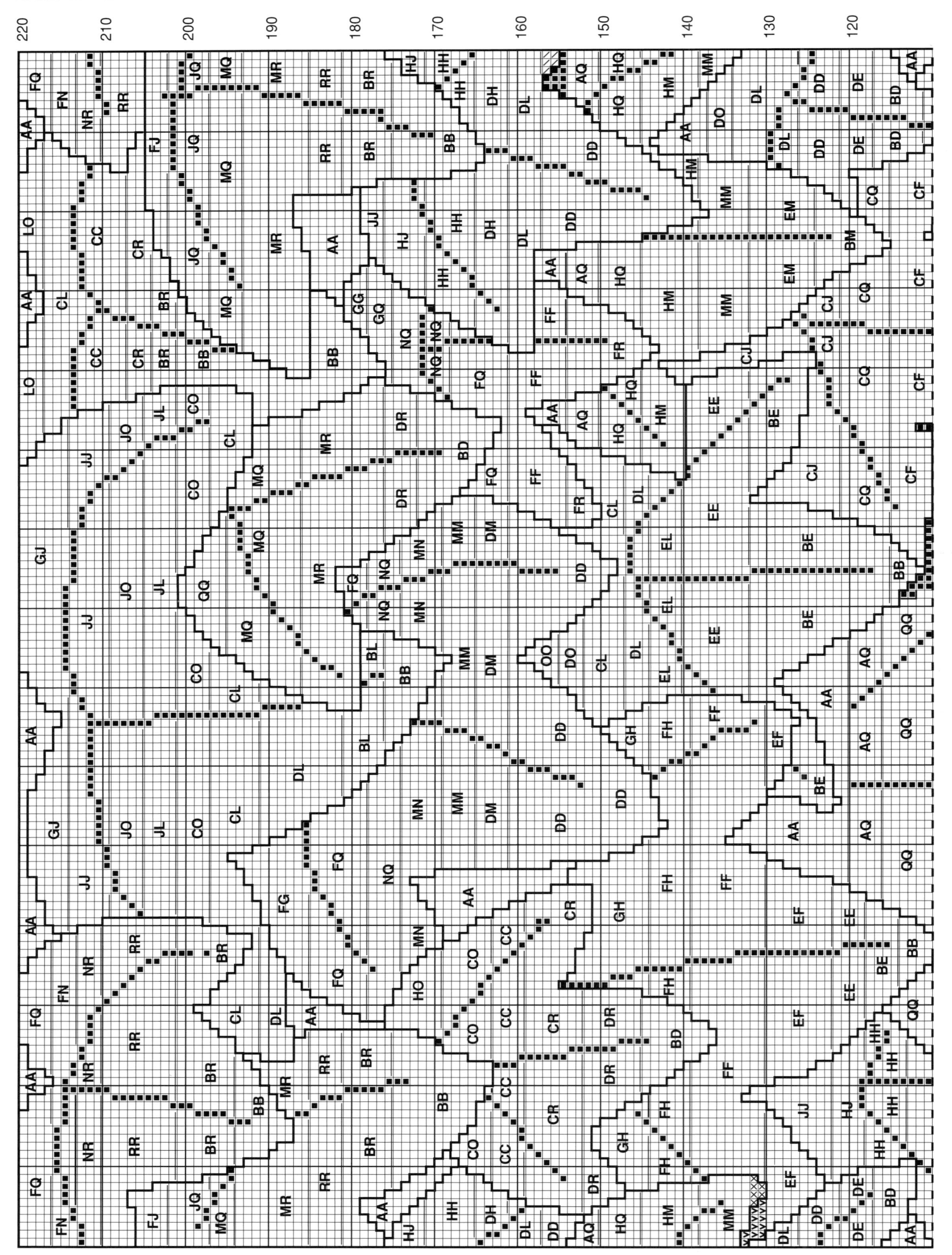

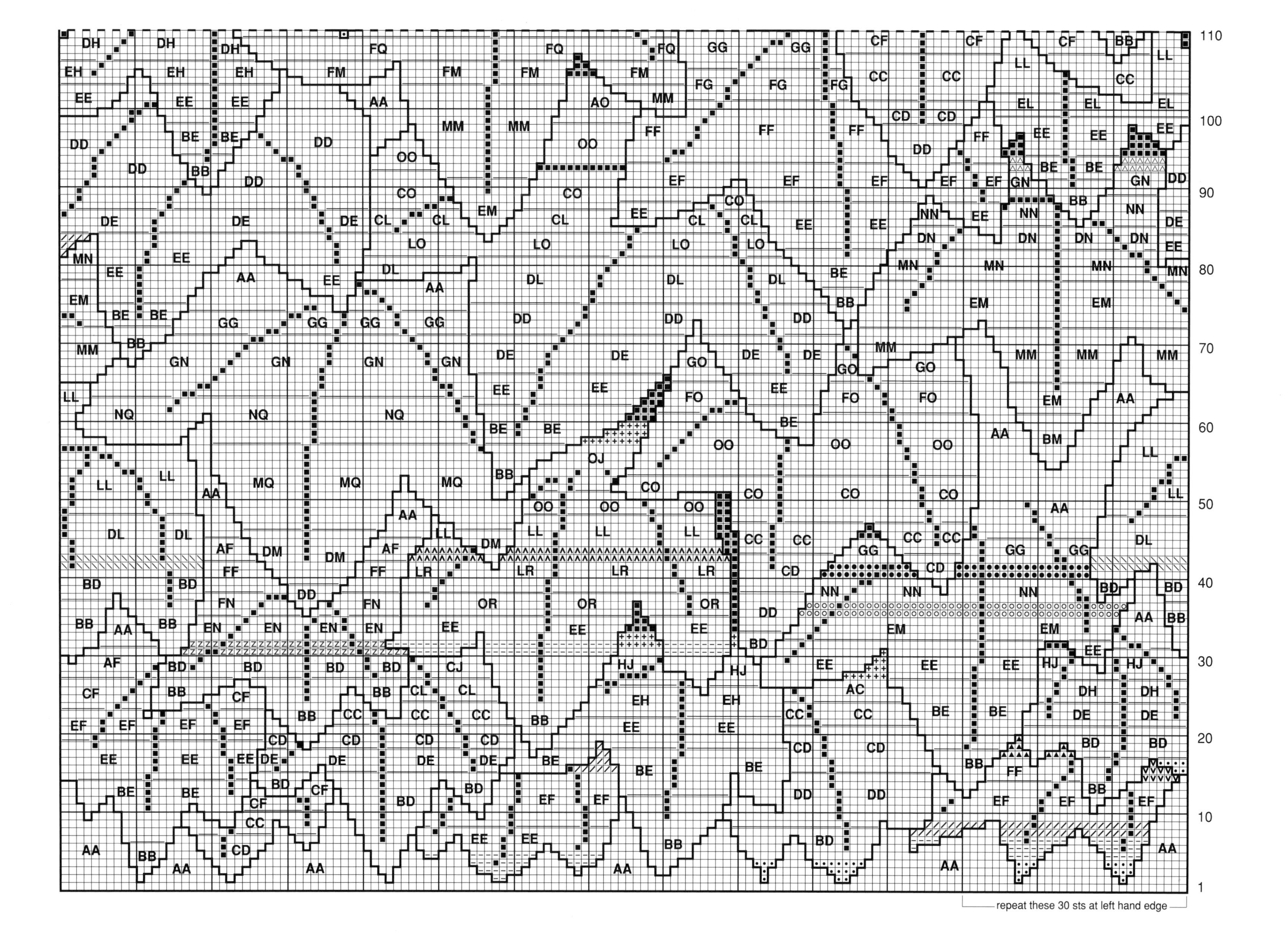
repeat these 30 sts at left hand edge

Border Chart

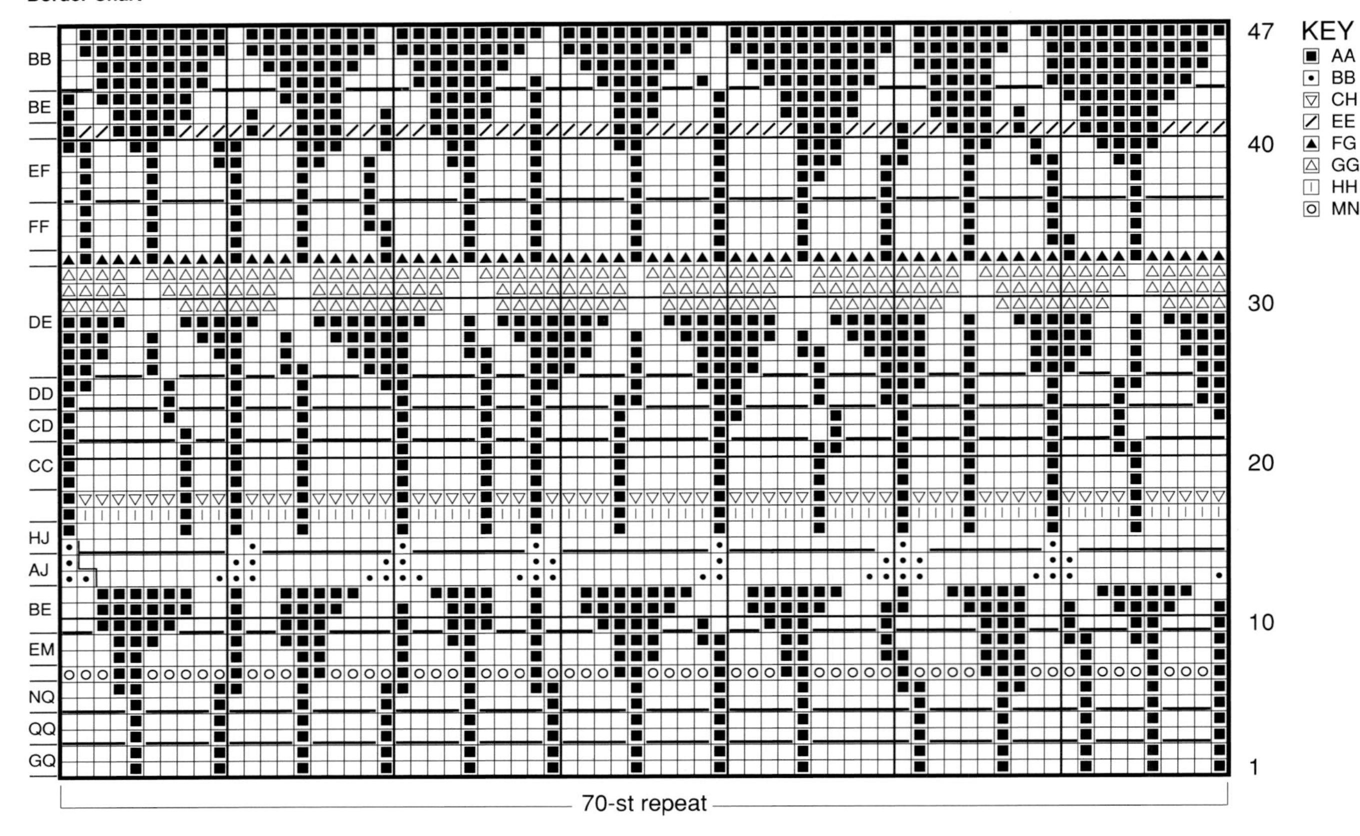

one strand of D used together, and so on. When working the colourwork pattern on the main piece of knitting, use a mixture of the Fair Isle and intarsia techniques. Use the intarsia method for working the individual leaves, using separate lengths of yarn for each striped leaf and linking one leaf to the next by twisting the yarns around each other on WS where they meet to avoid holes. Use the Fair Isle method for working colour AA (which is used for the background colour and for the veins on the leaves). Work AA across each row, carrying it loosely across the WS of the work when not in use and weaving it in every 3 or 4 sts to avoid long loose ends.

When working the colourwork pattern on the borders, use the Fair Isle method.

Read charts from right to left for k (RS odd-numbered) rows and from left to right for p (WS even-numbered) rows.

Main design

Using circular needle and a piece of waste yarn, cast on 180 sts. Break off waste yarn. Working back and forth in rows, beg charted colourwork pattern (shown on pages 122 and 123) as follows:

1st chart row (RS) Using AA, knit.

Mark each end of last row with a coloured thread.

2nd chart row (WS) Purling all sts and reading chart from left to right, work first 30 sts of chart first by working 7 AA, *1 BB, 13 AA, 1 BB, 8 AA,* then work all 150 sts of chart by working 10 AA, 1 BB, 11AA, 1 CD, 20 AA, 1 BD, 13 AA, 2 BE, 34 AA, 1 BB, 9 AA, 2 BB, 22 AA, then rep from * to * for last 23 sts.

3rd chart row Knitting all sts and reading chart from right to left, work all 150 sts of chart first by working *7 AA, 3 BB, 11AA, 2 BB,* 21 AA, 4 BB, 8 AA, 1 BB, 12 AA, 2 BB, 10 AA, 1 BE, 7 AA, 6 BE, 11 AA, 2 BD, 18 AA, 3 CD, 9 AA, 2 BB, 10 AA, then rep from * to * for next 23 sts, 7 AA.

This sets position of colourwork pattern.

Working first 30 sts of chart at end of every k row and at beg of every p row, cont in st st following chart until 220th chart row has been completed, so ending with a p row.

Mark each end of last row with a coloured thread.

Break off all yarns except AA.

Knitted borders

The top border is worked as a continuation of the main piece of knitting.

Top border

Using AA, knit one row.

★★**Next row** (WS) Using AA, p1, insert left-hand needle from front to back under horizontal strand between last stitch worked and next stitch on left-hand needle, forming a new loop on left-hand needle, then purl into back loop of this stitch – called *M1* –, purl to last st, M1, p1. (182 sts)

Beg colourwork pattern (shown on page 124) on next row as follows:

1st chart row (RS) Knitting all sts and reading chart from right to left, 1 GQ, using AA work M1, ★[3 GQ, 1 AA] twice, [4 GQ, 1 AA] twice, 6 GQ, [1 AA, 4 GQ] 9 times, 1 AA,★ rep from ★ to ★ once more, [3 GQ, 1 AA] twice, [4 GQ, 1 AA] twice, 6 GQ, [1 AA, 4 GQ] 3 times, 1 AA, using GQ work M1, 1 GQ. (184 sts)

This sets postion of colourwork pattern. Increasing one st at each end of every row as set and repeating 70-st repeat across each row (working all increased sts into patt), cont in st st following chart until 47th chart row has been completed, so ending with a k row.

Break off all yarns except AA.

Cont with AA only, p next row, then k one row inc one st at each end of row, and k 3 rows without shaping, so ending with a RS row. Cast (bind) off purlwise.★★

Bottom border

With RS facing and using circular needle, slip needle through first row of AA sts at cast-on edge, then remove waste yarn. (180 sts)

With WS facing, work as for top border from ★★ to ★★.

Side borders

With RS facing and using circular needle and AA, pick up and k 176 evenly along one side between coloured markers, picking up 4 sts for every 5 row ends.

Next row (WS) Using AA, p1, M1, purl to last st, M1, p1. (178 sts)

Beg colourwork pattern on next row as follows:

1st chart row (RS) Knitting all sts and reading chart from right to left, 1 GQ, using AA work M1, ★[3 GQ, 1 AA] twice, [4 GQ, 1 AA] twice, 6 GQ, [1 AA, 4 GQ] 9 times, 1 AA,★ rep from ★ to ★ once more, [3 GQ, 1 AA] twice, [4 GQ, 1 AA] twice, 6 GQ, [1 AA, 4 GQ] twice, 1 AA, 1 GQ, using GQ work M1, 1 GQ. (180 sts)

This sets postion of colourwork pattern. Increasing one st at each end of every row as set and repeating 70-st repeat across each row (working all increased sts into patt), cont in st st following chart until 47th chart row has been completed, so ending with a k row.

Break off all yarns except AA.

Cont with AA only, p next row, then k one row inc one st at each end of row, and k 3 rows without shaping, so ending with a RS row. Cast (bind) off purlwise.

Work second side border in same way as first. Join mitred corner seams.

Press lightly on WS with a damp cloth and a warm iron.

Crochet border

The simple crochet border is 3 rounds of double crochet (US single crochet). Note that the instructions are written using the UK terms for the stitches with the US terms in parentheses (see page 157 for a full explanation of the UK and the US crochet terminology).

Using the crochet hook and working in rounds with the RS always facing, begin the crochet border as follows:

1st rnd Using CJ, join the yarn with a slip st to one corner and work 1ch, 3dc(sc) into same place that slip st was worked, work dc(sc) evenly along first side, ★3dc(sc) in next corner, work dc(sc) evenly along next side,★ rep from ★ to ★ twice more, then using SS join with a slip st to first dc(sc) of rnd. Do not turn at end of rounds.

Break off CJ.

2nd rnd Using SS, work 1ch, 1dc(sc) into each dc(sc) and 3dc(sc) in each of 4 corners, then using TU join with a slip st to first dc(sc) of rnd. Break off SS.

3rd rnd Work as for 2nd rnd, but using TU. Fasten off. Do not press crochet edge.

Why is it that a collection of objects with the same theme take on a magic? Repetition of forms is part of the answer, as well as the amazing and impressive variety that can exist in a single generic group. Often quite ordinary objects become surprisingly special when surrounded by similar mates.

When I was invited to view an interesting country house recently, imagine my utter astonishment when I was led into a kitchen with a huge wall of fruit and veg in porcelain! The biggest Welsh dresser I had ever seen stood before me, laden with a veritable waterfall of tea pots, cream jugs, sugar bowls, plates and tureens in the form of my favourite fruits and vegetables. Among others, there were bunches of grapes, radishes, lettuces, oranges and apples – all fashioned as usable vessels. Most of the items in this collection are contemporary porcelains and it is lovely that we can collect such amusing pieces ourselves.

To see asparagus, cauliflower, artichokes, and celery used as dishes is to realize all over again what beautiful forms these everyday items possess. If I were restricted to vegetables and leaves as design motifs, I could happily work a lifetime on that subject matter without running dry. The opulant grace of the cabbage still delights me even though I have already designed cushions, table mats and carpets from its leafy form.

ABOVE: I designed this hanging for Marks and Spencer Christmas packaging. RIGHT: A veritable waterfall of fruit and vegetable porcelain.

ABOVE: My leafy painted mural in a tiled conservatory in Rye.

Sticking to my leaf theme, I painted the walls of a small conservatory in Rye with a desert garden. The inspiration was a painting by Adrian Allinson that I had included in my 1993 diary which had a leaf theme. I changed the colours somewhat to compliment the Rupert Spira tiles. Then, by adding a far off mountain scape and a cloudy sky, the tiny room took on an airy openness that is very pleasant to live in. Because I was starting from an existing painting I was able to work very swiftly. The mural was finished in a weekend.

The vivid mossy tones of my *Frog Cushion* act as a bright highlight in the soft grey green colour scheme of the conservatory. The frog can be stitched square or shaped.

flowers

Flowers can be delicately feminine, coolly elegant, coy and banal, or – as I have chosen to display them here – they can dance a tarantella making the senses drunk on their colourful dramatics. Probably my favourite approach to flowers is the gypsy madness of floral embroidery worked on flower prints which is then encrusted with beads and sequins. When Slavic peasants drape

themselves like Christmas trees with flower-embroidered costumes, then pose in front of furniture that is crawling with painted flowers, what a rich twinkling texture they present.

Another lusciously textured style that is now widely available, but none the less beautiful for that, is the one seen on the all-over flower-covered painted boxes, mirror frames, and bracelets from Kashmir. Densely studded with colourful blooms and leaves, these little gems light up many a Western lady's dressing table.

Thinking of flowers used in interiors reminds me of a recent visit to Venice where I had coffee in a famous old coffee house called Florian. The café's highly decorated walls are covered with framed panels of exquisite flower studies and painted figures. The backgrounds of all the paintings are

LEFT: The acid green *Nosegay Cushion* kit holding its own in opulent surroundings. OVERLEAF: The flowers drawing room gives a chance to see large-scale flowers in action. The one-off petit point *Rose Waistcoat/Vest* serves as a painting.

soft greys and browny-greys so that the flower colours quietly glow, giving this fabulous place a restrained old-world elegance. I was so struck by the soft and mellow effect of these framed studies covering the entire surface of each wall that I am recreating the same effect in my own hallway. I'll probably use deep lacquer red frames for my little pots of flowers. Topkapi Palace in Istanbul (see page 92) serves as another inspiration for panels of decorative flowers and fruits on walls.

One of my favourite examples of flower decoration to be found in England is in the roofed-in courtyard of Wallington Hall, a late-seventeenth-century mansion in the north of England. The courtyard walls are painted with landscape murals separated by tall rectangular border panels of life-sized, or larger, detailed portraits of flowering plants like thistles and sweet peas. I saw these sumptuously painted pillars quite a few years back, but like all works done with passion they have stayed in my memory.

One flower whose boldness attracts many designers is the sunflower. Think of all those Victorian flower paintings that featured this lion of a bloom, and of the splendid carved brick sunflower details on English buildings of the same period. Nineteenth-century tile panels too displayed memorable stylized versions of this tall leafy flower. If you want an

ABOVE: This marriage of roses and leaves comes closest to what this book is about for me. TOP: These flower-studded cloths and furniture in a Hungarian setting warm my heart.

exciting subject for a strong wall hanging or a high-backed chair, try this huge shaggy burst of gold with interesting circles of colour at its centre.

For years I have admired the pattern-filled work of the nineteenth-century French painter Édouard Vuillard. When I chose flowers as a theme for one of my rooms, his densely flowered *Figures and Interiors* sprang to mind. At first I thought I would make all the flower prints in the room small and intensely busy as Vuillard had done, but I later gravitated towards the larger-scale boldness of overblown roses, peonies and pansies. I suppose I wanted a chance to see an interior with large-scale blooms in order to measure the effect. For an atmosphere easier to live with day to day, I would probably settle for smaller-scale flowers, but it was exciting to play on this big scale. The effect did astound those who ventured into the electrifying room.

Once I settled on this operatically ripe mood, I went in search of wallpaper. I was delighted to find that Sanderson's London showroom still sported over-the-top large-scale flowered wallpapers and borders. I chose two colourways of the same rose paper. Then I glued extra cutout roses to the border for added embellishment.

ABOVE: *Figures and Interiors* (1896) by Édouard Vuillard is the painting that has haunted me for years and led to the interior on pages 132 and 133.

When I was collecting more objects for this interior, flower-covered china seemed to wink at me from flea-market stalls and Spanish and Chinese shawls leapt off antique-shop walls at me. The black rose-patterned pots I brought into the scene were particularly strong and reflect the hand-painted black rose and ribbon chest of drawers. My collection of bold flowery beaded bags and bright fans add gorgeous intense areas of detail to the room. That yellow hat box in the flower scene is begging to be translated into a textile design, don't you think?

Made especially for my flowers room, the *Flowers Rag Rug* was inspired by old American rag rugs I saw at the American Museum in Bath. There were several there with dark blue and tobacco brown grounds that had strong borders and large primitive central red roses. I started my rag rug just before Christmas and finished it seven days later. It is a perfect project for winter days spent at home with family. Keeps you out of squabbles wonderfully!

The large flowers on my rug are constructed like those on oriental embroidery and primitive paintings of roses; each petal starts with a deep-coloured centre and shades out to the lightest colour at the petal's edge. The leaves in the border have a simple structure. Each one is begun with a brilliant bilious or dark-coloured vein, then a deep centre is worked, followed by lighter edges. The pansies and round flowers are also shaded from dark to light.

The inky background on the rug is worked in many shades of navy, bright blue, charcoal, black, dark tweed, bottle green and a few patches of purple. It is critical before hooking the ground to keep a vision of how that dark background will effect each element of design. When surrounded with empty hessian a flower can look awkward and garish, but once the navy ground is hooked around it that same flower will

ABOVE: The rose chest of drawers painted by Jill Gordon houses my collection of rosy china and the dark *Nosegay Cushion*. RIGHT: The back of the *Rose Chair* is covered with my fabric called *Marquetry*.

bloom into life like a light in the dark. The turquoise leaves attached to the flowers add a unity to the multiplicity of colours.

The inspiration for my needlepoint *Flower Fan Cushion* is an old painted fan I found in a flea market. The spontaneously painted soft slightly 'off' colours on the fan remind me of 1920s cosmetic boxes. The airforce grey ground on the needlepoint gives a special quality to the chalky pastels.

Continuing to add flower patterned objects to the room, I made the *Flower Collage Screen* which was exciting to compose. Arranging the diamond-shaped flower prints, paintings, wrapping papers, postcards and wallpapers in horizontal stripes gave a bit of order to the kaleidoscopic madness. Once I had covered the *Flowers Collage Screen* with the diamonds, I chose four cutout rose clusters to superimpose on the collage at the centre top of each panel. This detail softens the geometric repeat pattern.

The design for the pink *Rose Chair* grew from the necessity to give unskilled stitchers a job. I decided on a large central motif that would have miles of brocade background. The larger-than-life roses and sprawling leaves were executed by expert needlepointers, while most of the background was done by inexperienced volunteers. I like this chair better than some of my massively detailed pieces. The brocade ground drawn in a deliberately primitive manner is charming.

ABOVE: My watercolour of passionate overblown roses. LEFT: The *Rose Chair* in front of the *Flower Collage Screen.* The diamond cutout shape on the collage screen unifies a disparate array of flowers.

Flowers Collage Screen

Materials

- Screen or other foundation for collage
- Strong paper glue
- Small piece of cardboard
- Selection of flower cutouts from gift-wrapping paper, magazines, wallpaper and postcards
- Ochre acrylic and paint brush (optional)

Applying the collage cutouts

Cut a diamond-shaped piece of the desired size out of the centre of the piece of cardboard, leaving the cardboard frame around the diamond shape intact. Make sure all four sides of the diamond on the cardboard template are exactly equal in length or the collage cutouts will not fit together. Place the template over a flowered paper scrap and move it around until you have framed the flower motif in the desired way. Holding the template firmly in place, trace the diamond shape on to the paper. After tracing diamond shapes in this way on to your collection of flower scraps, cut out the paper diamonds.

Starting at the top of one section of the screen, arrange a few of the collage cutouts. Stand back to study the arrangement, then glue these first pieces in place. Continue in this way, working downwards. (See page 153 for more detailed instructions for collage techniques.)

Cover each section of the screen in the same way with diamond-shaped cutouts.

Finishing the screen

Glue one flower motif cutout to the centre of the top of each section of the screen.

Then, if desired, glaze the entire collage with an ochre acrylic wash.

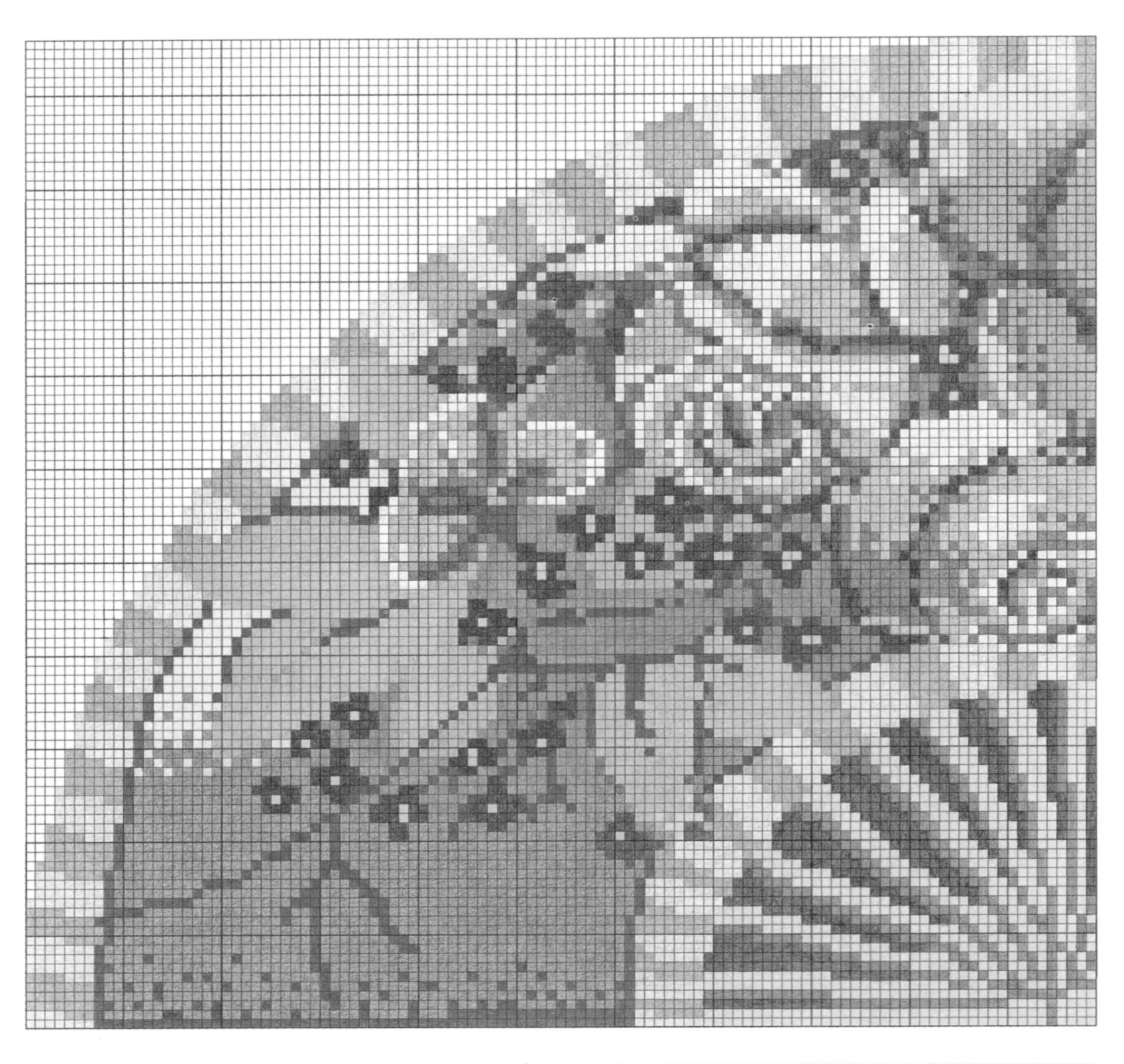

ABOVE: The *Flower Fan Cushion* can be backed with any fabric that suits your interior. You can see from the fan source that I heightened the colours in the needlepoint.

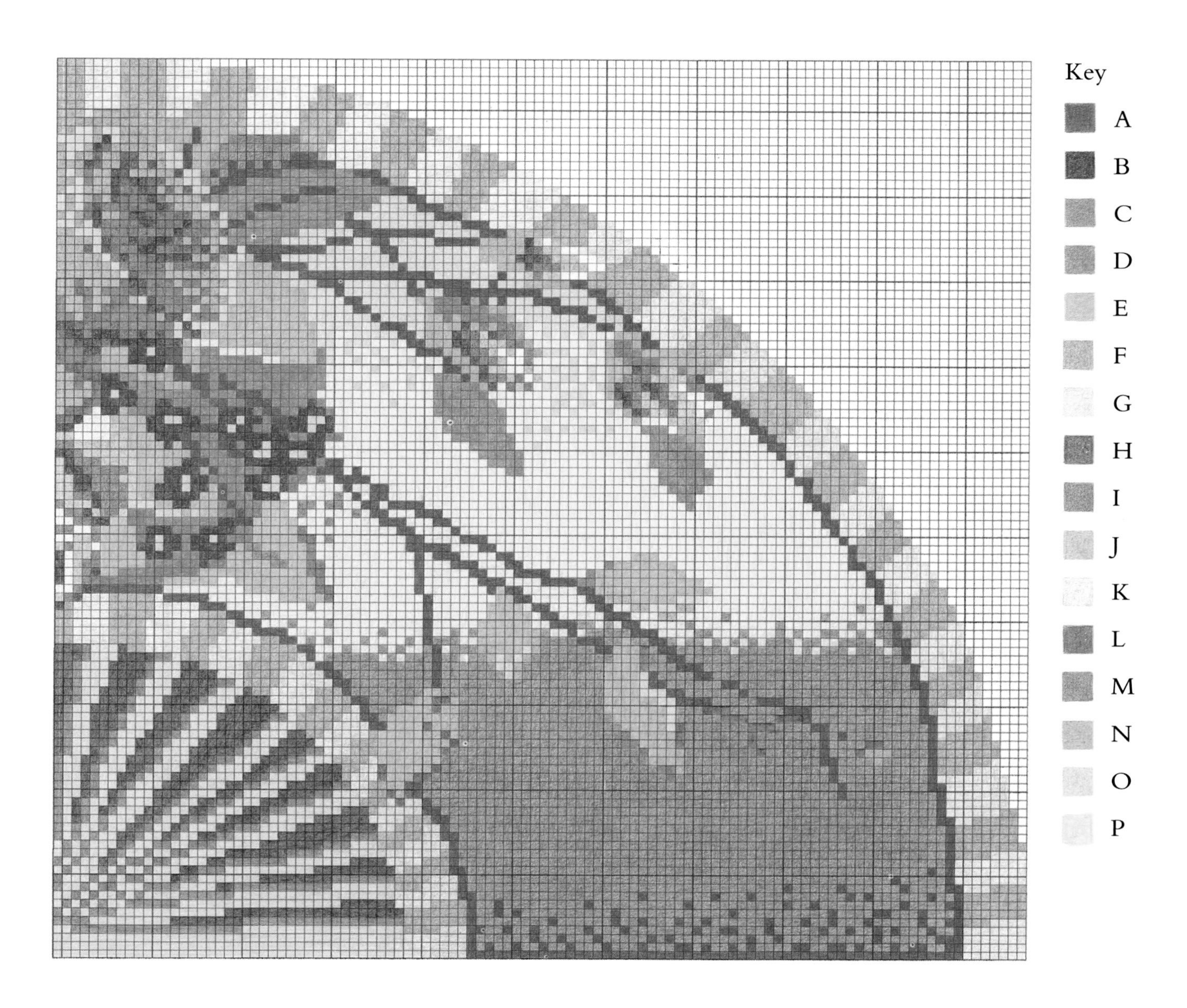

Flower Fan Cushion

Size of cushion

The finished shaped cushion measures 54cm (21½in) wide by 26cm (10½in) tall.

Materials

- 10-mesh single- or double-thread canvas 69cm (27in) by 41cm (16in)
- ANCHOR wool tapestry yarn in the 16 colours listed on the right
- Size 18 tapestry needle
- 50cm (½yd) of 90cm (36in) wide backing fabric and matching sewing thread
- 46cm (18in) zipper
- Cushion pad (pillow form) in shape of finished needlepoint and 6cm (2½in) thick

Yarn colours and amounts

You will need Anchor wool tapestry yarn (10m/11yd skeins) in the following 16 colours and approximate amounts:

A	Deep gobelin green	8884	3 skeins
B	Dark cornflower blue	8692	2 skeins
C	Mid sea green	8900	5 skeins
D	Peacock green	8920	2 skeins
E	Light apple green	9096	3 skeins
F	Sky blue	8820	3 skeins
G	Periwinkle	8602	3 skeins
H	Cyclamen	8442	2 skeins
I	Fuchsia	8456	1 skein
J	Light magenta	8482	2 skeins
K	Pale brick	9612	1 skein
L	Paprika	8234	1 skein
M	Dark autumn tints	9536	2 skeins
N	Mid autumn tints	9534	1 skein
O	Light autumn gold	8058	3 skeins
P	Pale leaf green	9192	3 skeins

Working the embroidery

The chart is 217 stitches wide and 106 stitches tall. Begin by marking the outline of the rectangular chart on to your canvas and, if desired, dividing the rectangle into tens

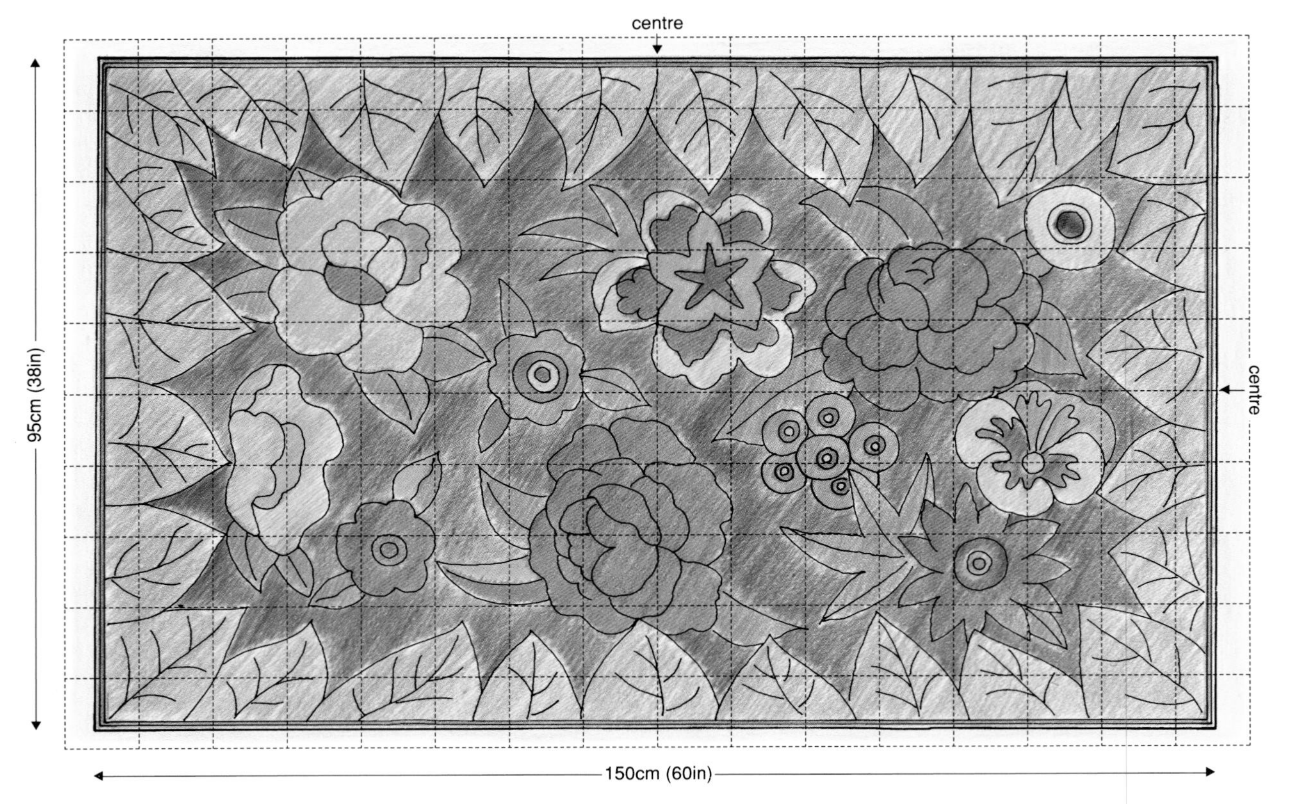

Note: Each square on the grid represents 10cm (4in).

just like the charted design. Make a paper template of the rectangular outline and set aside to use later as a guide for blocking.

Following the chart on pages 138 and 139, work the embroidery in tent stitch, using one strand of Anchor wool tapestry yarn (see page 150 for tent stitch techniques).

Finishing the cushion cover

After the embroidery has been completed, block the canvas, using the paper template as your guide (see page 152).

Trim the canvas edges, leaving a seam allowance of 2cm (3/4in).

Cut one piece of backing fabric the same size as the blocked and trimmed canvas. Then cut two strips of fabric for the gusset that fits around the edge of the needlepoint. One strip should be 10cm (4in) wide and the same length as the straight edge of the back and the other 10cm (4in) wide and long enough to fit along the curved edge.

Sew the longer strip to the curved edge of the needlepoint and the shorter strip to the straight edge, then join the corner seams. Sew the back to the gusset, inserting the zipper along the straight edge of the cover.

Flowers Rag Rug

Size of rag rug

The finished rag rug measures 95cm (38in) wide by 150cm (60in) long.

Materials

- Piece of loose-weave hessian (burlap) at least 111cm (44in) by 166cm (66in)
- Variety of scrap fabrics for strips
- Large rug hook
- 5.3m (5 3/4yd) of 6cm (2 1/2in) wide twilled carpet binding tape (optional)
- Strong thread for hemming

Choosing the colours

You will need scrap fabrics in a variety of colours and in a range of tones. Study the photograph of the rug for an idea of the types of colours to choose. Then look for scraps to fit into this scheme or to fit into your own original palette. (See page 147 for information on types of fabrics suitable for rag rugs.)

Transferring the design

Using a dressmaker's marking pen, mark the outer outline of the rug on to the right side

ABOVE: This rug echoes the primitive flowers on dark grounds of rags rugs at the American Museum in Bath that inspired it.

of the hessian (burlap). The dimensions of the outer outline are given on the previous page under *Size of rag rug* and are shown on the rug design diagram. Allow at least 8cm (3in) of extra fabric all around the edge for hemming.

Following the rug diagram at the top of the previous page, transfer the rag rug design on to the right side of the hessian (burlap) as instructed on page 148.

Preparing the rag strips

Cut some of the fabric scraps into strips 1.5cm (1/2in) to 2.5cm (1in) wide, depending on the thickness of the fabric. Cut only enough strips to provide a variety of tones and shades for working the first flower. Cut the remaining scraps only when you need them as the work progresses. A detailed explanation of how to cut strips for rag rugs is given with the rag rug techniques on page 148.

Hooking the rug

Before starting to hook the rag rug, read the hooking instructions on page 149.

Then begin the rag rug by working the large flowers at the centre of the design, using rag strips of the desired colour. (As a guideline, the rug diagram indicates some of the colours used on the original *Flowers Rag Rug*.)

After completing the flowers at the centre of the rag rug design, work two rows of loops in contrasting colours all around the outer outline of the rug. Then work the large leaves around the border, leaving the background until last.

Finishing the rug

After the hooking has been completed, bind the edges of the hessian (burlap) if desired, then turn back the edges and work the hem, mitring the corners. Turn to page 149 for finishing instructions.

ABOVE: Eighteenth-century floral wallpaper in Nostell Priory, Yorkshire. ABOVE LEFT: The *Auricula Slippers* in dusty tones. RIGHT: Oriental wallpaper and ceramic garden stools cheer up this hallway scene.

After the strong contrasts of blacks, reds, yellows and blues of the flowers sitting room, I wanted to try a cooler approach to this theme. I started the flowers hallway with the *Bowl of Pansies Cushion* and built the colour scheme from that pink, pale green and lavender palette.

Pansies are a gift to needlepoint artists. Their flat faces, contrasting bold colours and circular shapes are easy to depict and joyful to behold. I found a painted box, with a well-designed arrangement of pansies on a dark background, in a junk shop in Bath. I replaced the old ochre ground with a fresh milky green one to create the *Bowl of Pansies Cushion* (see page 144).

This hall is papered with a delightful oriental garden wallpaper mural from Alexander Beauchamp. The colourway I chose is cool grey-blue, but there is another with a soft duck-egg blue which is also very appealing. Every time I open my hall door I feel a rush of delight at the sight of what was a mundane rather dark hall, now transformed into this fanciful oriental garden.

I was once commissioned to do a needlepoint chair and showed the client the back when it was half finished. She said she wanted something 'far less pastel' with more pronounced reds. Never one to waste an effort, I finished the back and made it into the *Peony Cushion* that sits in my flowers hallway. You can see that the flowers on the cushion are composed of bright outlines with blushes of colour in each petal. The background for these blooms is several shades of maroon, burnt orange and deep pink, with dark lavender tones at the centre of the 'bouquet'.

Auriculas are another deliciously easy flower to capture in needlepoint. All you have to do is create a pale centre, then follow this immediately with a dark circle and shade gently out to light edges. The antique colourings of some auriculas make for elegant and tweedy slippers indeed. Seeing the needlepoint shoes photographed on the old painted table with begonia leaves (above left) makes me feel the same subject could make a stunning cushion, chair or mirror frame for a room in this antique palette. Auriculas also come in burnt oranges, deep claret reds and lemon yellows, so are often used in some very sparky colour schemes.

ABOVE: A nostalgic mood permeates this *Bowl of Pansies* kit sitting next to its tin-box source.

Bowl of Pansies Cushion

Size of cushion

The finished cushion measures 42cm (16½in) wide by 43cm (17in) tall.

Materials

- 10-mesh single- or double-thread canvas 56cm (22in) square
- APPLETON wool tapestry yarn in the 16 colours listed below
- Size 18 tapestry needle
- 70cm (¾yd) of 90cm (36in) wide backing fabric and matching sewing thread
- 1.8m (2yd) of piping (filling) cord or ready-made cord (optional)
- 33cm (13in) zipper
- Cushion pad (pillow form) same size as finished cover or slightly larger

Yarn colours and amounts

You will need Appleton wool tapestry yarn (10m/11yd skeins) in the following 16 colours and approximate amounts:

A	Deep brown grounding	583	1 skein
B	Dark autumn yellow	479	2 skeins

Key
A
B
C
D
E
F
G
H
I
J
K
L
M
N
O
P

ABOVE: For the ambitious, this 8-mesh pastel *Peony Cushion* shouldn't be too difficult to copy.

C	Light brown olive	311	2 skeins
D	Bright yellow	552	2 skeins
E	Dark English green	548	3 skeins
F	Mid English green	546	2 skeins
G	Light grass green	253	3 skeins
H	Pale leaf green	422	15 skeins
I	Light cornflower blue	462	2 skeins
J	Pale cornflower blue	461	7 skeins
K	Mid purple	105	2 skeins
L	Light purple	102	2 skeins
M	Dark dull rose pink	147	2 skeins
N	Mid bright rose pink	944	1 skeins
O	Light rose pink	753	2 skeins
P	Off white	992	3 skeins

Working the embroidery

The chart is 165 stitches wide and 171 stitches tall. Begin by marking the outline of the design on to your canvas and, if desired, dividing it into tens just like the charted design. Make a paper template of the design outline and set aside to use later as a guide for blocking.

Following the chart on pages 144 and 145, work the embroidery in tent stitch, using one strand of Appleton wool tapestry yarn (see page 150 for stitch techniques). Leave the background (pale leaf green, shade no. 422) until last.

Finishing the cushion cover

After the embroidery has been completed, block the canvas, using the paper template as your guide (see page 152).

Trim the canvas edges, leaving a seam allowance of 2cm (3/4in).

Sew the zipper between two pieces of fabric for the cushion cover back as instructed on page 152.

If desired, cover the piping (filling) cord and pin to the needlepoint. Then join the front and back of the cover as described on page 152. If you are using a ready-made cord as a trimming, sew it to the completed cover, tucking the ends into a small opening in the seam.

Techniques

Here are some useful tips for making the projects set out in this book. To my usual repertoire of knitting and needlepoint I have added rag rugs, mosaics and collage. Hopefully, these crafts will make my designs accessible to those who find knitting and needlepoint too time-consuming or too difficult. More importantly, by introducing you to more media that enthral me, I hope, as ever, to inspire you to strike out on your own designs.

The hints outlined below are the ones I find really useful myself. I wouldn't want to lay down strict or rigid rules for any of the techniques outlined. The main thing is to learn the basic skills and pick up those little tips that make it easier. With a tiny bit of practice any given technique will then just flow effortlessly and you can get on with the real joy of all decorative art – playing with patterns and colours and creating dazzling designs.

Rag Rugs

Don't be deterred from trying to make a rag rug by its size. Because of the large individual loops and the simple hooking action used to form them, rag rugs are very quick to work. The basic techniques that follow couldn't be simpler.

Rag fabrics

The materials that go into a rag rug are a good selection of scrap fabrics for your rag strips and a large piece of hessian (burlap) for the rug foundation.

Most fabric scraps are suitable for rag rugs. Finding fabric scraps shouldn't be a problem. You can save old clothes or pick up cheap old cast-offs at car boot or jumble sales or even thrift shops. Rag rugs are the ultimate way to recycle.

Patterned fabrics are just as good to work with as plain and they sometimes give a lovely mottled effect. Don't restrict your choice of fabrics to a specific thickness or texture either. Varying textures and fabric weights will just add interest to the all-over design and keep it from being too uniform. I tend to collect fabrics that will go well with a specific palette. But try to find a wide enough variety of colours and in a range of dark, medium and light tones. If you have a good selection to hand, you will be able to pick and choose suitable colours as your design progresses.

Foundation fabric

Hessian (burlap) is the best foundation for looped rag rugs. It provides a strong base and the threads are wide apart enough to accommodate the rug hook. I usually use a heavy-weight, loose weave hessian which has about 10 or 11 threads to the inch. Be sure to purchase a piece of hessian which is at least 7.5cm (3in) bigger all around than the size of your finished rug.

Rug hooks

The main piece of equipment you will need for working a rag rug is, of course, a rug hook. There are two types of rug hook – one with a latchet and one without. I prefer working with a latchet rug hook because it is so easy to use. The latchet is pushed upwards when the hook is inserted down through the fabric and downwards over the rag strip as the hook is pulled up through the fabric. This avoids the possibility of catching the hook in the hessian as it is pulled through.

Rug frames

I work my rag rugs in the hand without a frame. This allows me to carry my rag rug project around with me and allows me to jump around the design filling in various areas without having to reframe it each time. My finished rugs might not be as absolutely rectangular as a rug worked in a frame, but this slight asymmetry is part of the charm of the hand-hooked rag rug. If you do want to use a frame, you could improvise a frame rather than go to the expense of buying a large rug frame. A good sized artist's stretcher frame will do the trick. Use drawing pins (thumb tacks) to secure the section of hessian you are working on to the stretcher.

Transferring designs

The instructional diagrams for my rag rugs are drawn on a grid divided into squares each of which represents a square measuring 10cm (4in) by 10cm (4in). The design outlines must be enlarged square for square following the diagram. You can either draw the enlarged design directly on to the hessian foundation or on to tracing paper. A design drawn on to tracing paper can be later transferred to the hessian by using a hot-iron transfer pencil.

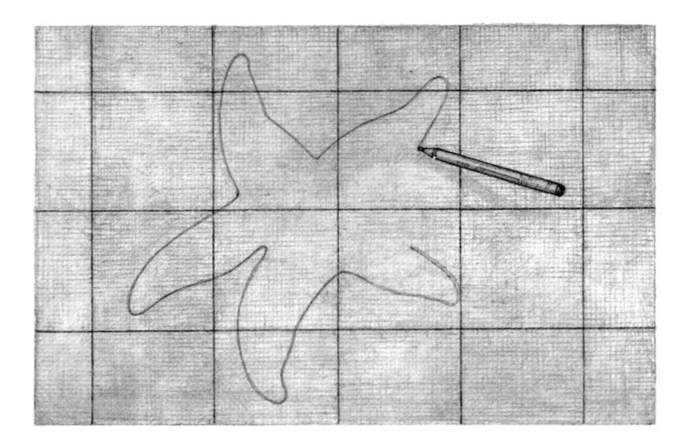

If you are drawing directly on to the hessian, begin by drawing the outer outline of the rug using a dressmaker's felt-tip pen and following the dimensions given on the diagram. Then draw the grid exactly as it is on the diagram beginning with the centre horizontal and vertical lines and then positioning the remaining grid lines 10cm (4in) apart.

Following the diagram, copy the design outlines, completing the lines in one square before moving on to the next. When drawing the design directly on to the hessian, use a contrasting coloured pen so that the design outlines can be easily distinguished from the grid. Don't worry about mistakes, as they will be covered up by the loops.

If you are enlarging the design on to tracing paper use a pencil to draw the outline and grid. To transfer the design from the tracing paper, first turn the paper over and with a transfer pencil retrace the outer outline of the rug and the design outlines (not the grid). Place the tracing paper on the hessian with the transfer pencil side facing the right side of the hessian. Then using a hot iron, press the design on to the hessian following the instructions that come with the transfer pencil.

Preparing the rag strips

It is a good idea to wash and dry all your scrap fabrics before cutting them into strips. This will ensure that all your fabrics are pre-shrunk before use. You might even want to dye some of your scraps beforehand if you have been unable to find some of the colours you need.

There is no hard and fast rule about how wide to cut the rag strips. The strip width depends on several factors: the type of texture you want, the thickness of the fabric, the size of your rug hook and the weight of your hessian foundation. The best thing to do is to cut a short strip of a particular fabric and test it. In fact, it is never a good idea to cut all your fabric into strips before you begin your rag rug. You should only cut strips as your work progresses. As a general rule of thumb I cut my rag strips between 1.5cm (½in) and 2.5cm (1in) wide – the thicker the fabric is the narrower the strip should be.

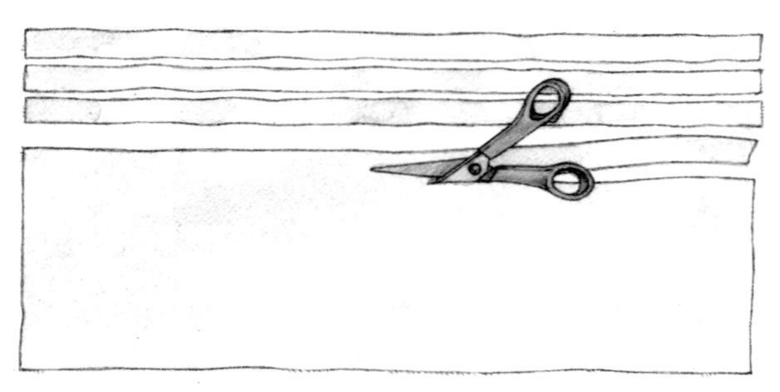

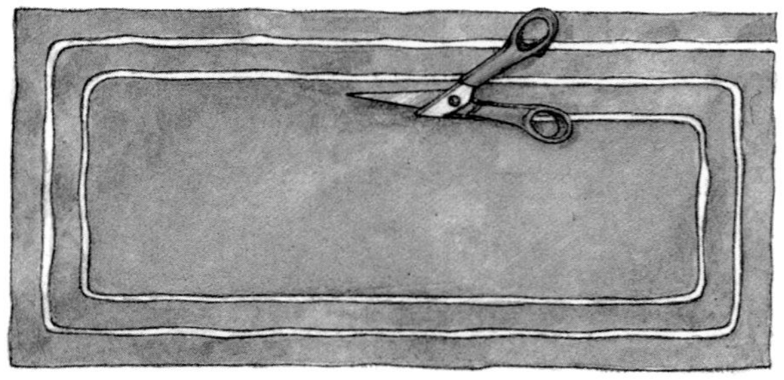

Cut strips on the straight grain of the fabric and not on the bias. For a long continuous strip, cut round and round towards the middle of the piece of fabric as shown above.

Hooking

Learning to hook a rag rug will take no time at all, especially if your use a latchet hook.

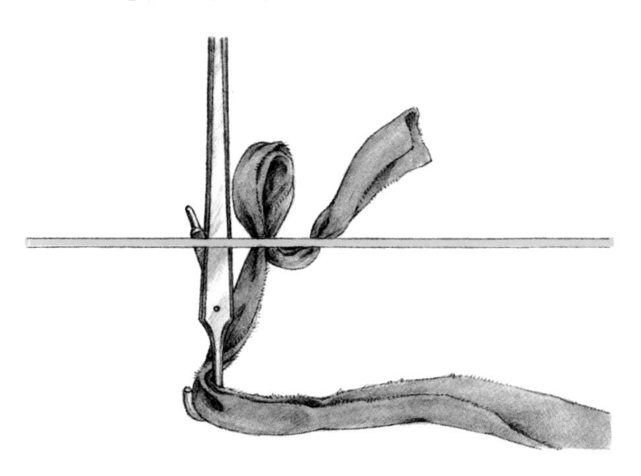

If you are right-handed hold the hook in your right hand above the hessian and hold the rag strip in your left hand under the hessian. Push the hook straight down through the hessian. Catch the fabric strip with the hook and pull the end of the strip through. Then insert the hook through the hessian one or two fabric threads away from where it was first inserted. Pull the fabric strip through again, this time forming a loop on the right side of the hessian. Continue making loops in this way, packing the loops close together but not over tightly. My rugs generally have about 7 loops to 5cm (2in).

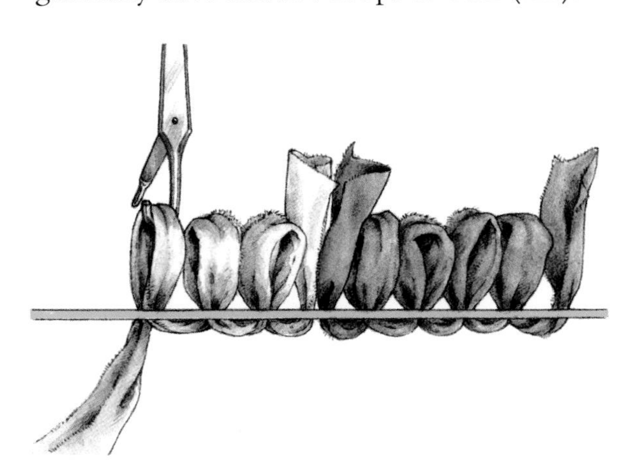

To finish off a strip (or change colours) merely pull the end through to the right side. Start the next strip about two fabric thread away from where the last strip ended. Do not insert the hook through the exact same hole as a previous loop or strip end or you might pull out a loop by accident. Trim the ends of the strips to the same level as the loops.

The direction of working the loops is a matter of choice. It usually follows the shape of the design. For instance, on my *Celebration Squares Rag Rug* (page 26) the loops are worked in straight lines, but curved shapes can be filled in with loops at random or in curves that follow the shape.

If you have never made a rag rug before, practise hooking on a spare piece of hessian to test your strip widths and to decide on the height of the loops. You will find that you can pull the loops out if you make a mistake. After a completed rug has been walked on it will be much harder to pull the loops out because the flattening of the rug pushes the loops tighter together.

Finishing rag rugs

A special advantage of rag rug making is that very little finishing is required. After completing the hooking, simply turn under the unworked hessian all around the edge and hem, mitring the corners in the process. Alternatively trim the unworked hessian to 4cm (1½in) and sew on a 6cm (2½in) wide twilled carpet binding close to the loops. Then turn the tape to the wrong side and sew in place with a strong thread.

Needlepoint

Working tent stitch on canvas is so easy that anyone can pick it up in just a few minutes with the help of an enthusiastic stitcher. Learning from a book may take a little longer, but it's well worth the effort.

Needlepoint canvas

Needlepoint is worked on an evenweave canvas. The canvas comes in various mesh sizes, ranging from the finest with 32 holes or threads per 2.5cm (1in) to the coarsest with 3 holes per 2.5cm (1in). Then finer meshes are used for the very tiny tent stitches called petit point and the coarser for carpets. I generally prefer using 10-mesh or 8-mesh canvas. These two sizes give me a stitch size that is small enough to create the detail I want, but big enough to get a quick result.

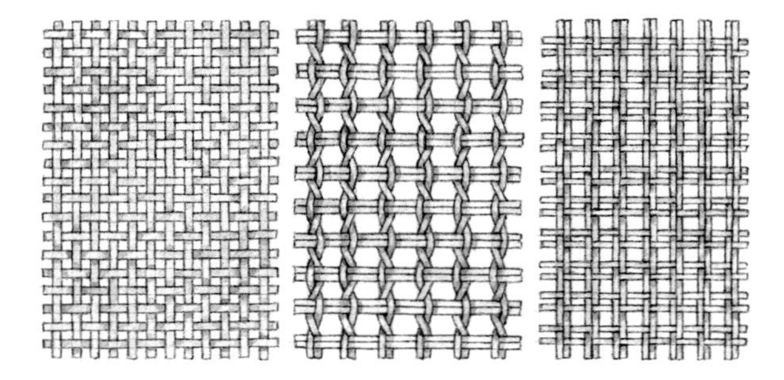

Needlepoint canvas comes in three different types – single-thread (or mono) canvas (above left), interlocked canvas (above centre) and double-thread (or Penelope) canvas (above right). The finest canvas sizes are generally only available in single-thread canvas and the coarsest in interlocked canvas. The middle range of sizes come in all three types.

Which type of canvas you use is up to you. I like working on double-thread canvas because you can work all types of stitches on it, including the half-cross tent stitch technique (see page 151). Also, it is usually softer than the other types, because it is not as stiff as interlocked or single-thread canvas and because the individual threads are finer than those of a single-thread canvas of the same gauge.

Interlocked canvas has threads which are locked together so it does not fray or distort during stitching as much as the two other types.

When buying canvas remember to allow for a minimum of 5cm (2in) extra unworked canvas all around the design.

Needlepoint yarns

Needlepoint yarn comes in various thicknesses. The thing to watch out for is that the yarn must be thick enough to cover the canvas threads but not so thick that it needs to be forced through the holes.

The standard wool needlepoint yarn weights are crewel, Persian and tapestry. Crewel yarn is quite fine and at least three strands used together are needed for a 10-mesh canvas. The advantage of the finer yarns is that you can 'mix' your own colours by using up to three different shades to create your own original tones for a 10-mesh needlepoint canvas.

Wool tapestry yarn is thicker than crewel yarn and a single strand will cover a 10-mesh canvas, and two strands a 7- or 8-mesh canvas.

Persian yarn is made up of three strands of yarn that can be easily separated. Each of these single strands is slightly thicker than crewel yarn. (See page 157 for more information on needlepoint yarns.)

Needlepoint stitches

There are many types of needlepoint stitches. I tend to use only two types of stitches – tent stitch or random long stitch. I find these stitches quick and easy to work and they give the type of texture I like for my designs.

Because I carry my needlepoint with me everywhere, I like working needlepoint handheld, instead of stretched on to an embroidery frame. I personally also find the stitching easier to manipulate when working in the hand. Some stitchers prefer working with an embroidery frame because it leaves two hands free and keeps the canvas from being distorted by the stitches. The only way to decide which is best for you is to try both!

The needlepoint projects with complete instructions in this book are all worked in tent stitch, so instructions for tent stitch are given below. There are three methods for working tent stitch and they all look the same on the front of the canvas. Only the back looks different. I often use all three techniques – half-cross, continental, and basketweave – on the same canvas! For large solid backgrounds, however, it is best to stick to just one tent-stitch technique to avoid creating visible ridges on the right side of your finished needlepoint.

Continental tent stitch

Before beginning to work tent stitch, select a blunt-ended tapestry needle large enough to hold the yarn without damaging it, but not so large that it has to be forced through the needlepoint canvas. Be sure not to use too long a piece of yarn – 30cm (15in) is plenty. If your needlepoint yarn is too long it will twist and tangle and slow you down.

Continental tent stitch can be worked on any type of needlepoint canvas – single-thread, double-thread or interlocked. It produces a solidly covered surface on the back of the work.

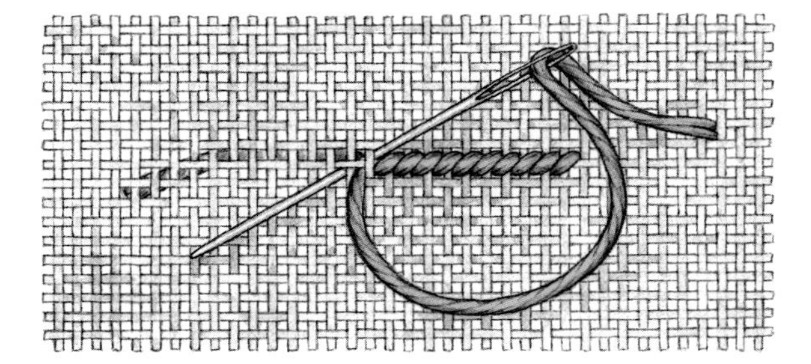

Leave a 2.5cm (1in) long loose end of yarn at the back of the needlepoint canvas and work the first few tent stitches from right to left over it as shown above.

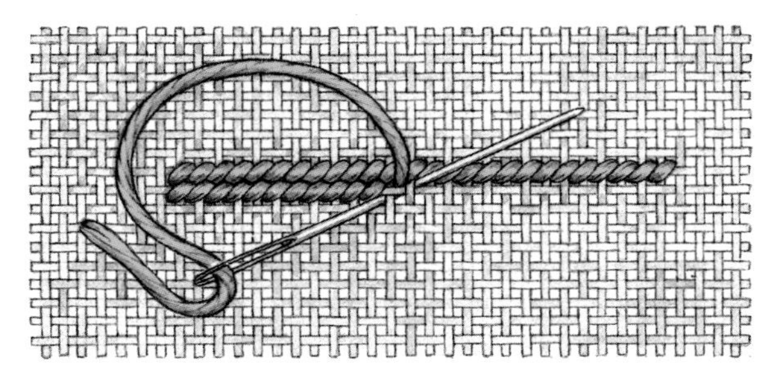

Work the following rows of stitches below the first row. To fasten off the end of a length of yarn pass it through a few stitches at the back of the canvas.

Basketweave tent stitch

Like continental tent stitch, basketweave tent stitch can be worked on any type of canvas. It is a good technique to use for covering large solid backgrounds because it tends to keep the canvas from biasing.

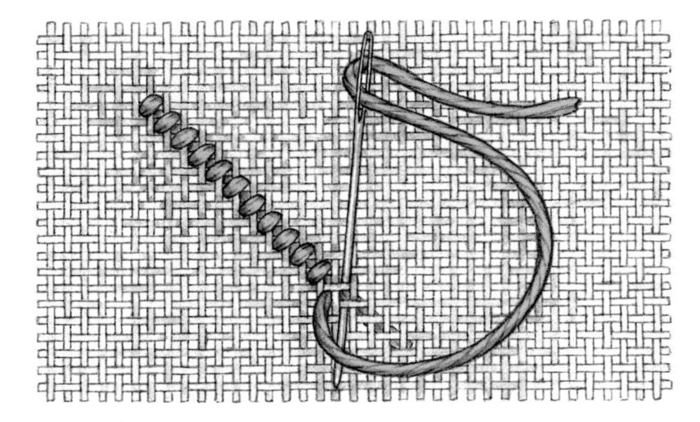

Working the first few stitches over the loose end at the back as for continental tent stitch, work the first row downwards diagonally from left to right, forming vertical stitches at the back.

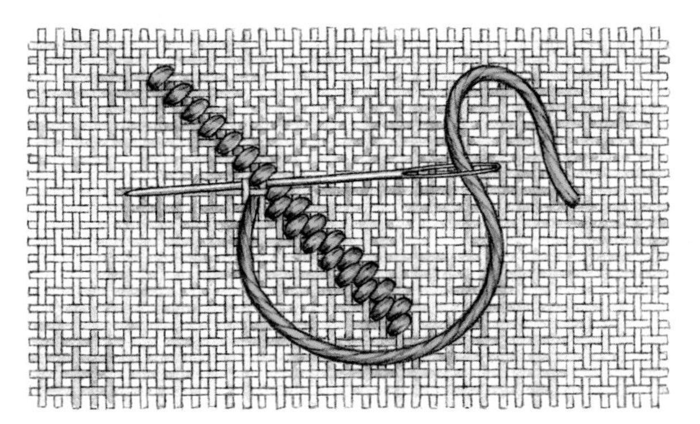

Work the following row upwards from right to left, slotting in between the stitches of the previous row and forming horizontal stitches at the back. Repeat the downward and upward rows alternately. Fasten off as for continental tent stitch.

Half-cross tent stitch

The half-cross technique uses less yarn than the other two tent stitch techniques. This is because the stitches at the back of the work are short, vertical stitches that do not cover the back of the canvas. When an entire design is worked in half-cross stitch the resulting needlepoint is not as thick as a needlepoint worked in one of the other two techniques. Half cross stitch requires double-thread or interlocked canvas and cannot be worked on single-thread canvas.

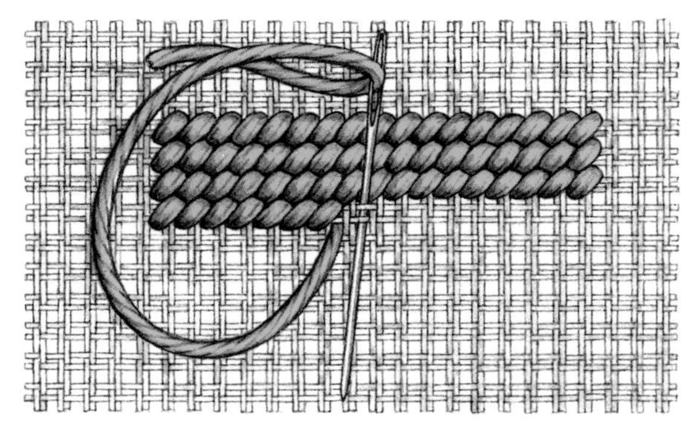

When beginning half-cross tent stitch, work over the loose end at the back (see continental tent stitch). Work in rows alternately from left to right and right to left, making short vertical stitches at the back as shown above. Fasten off the end of a length of yarn as for continental tent stitch.

Needlepoint charts

The instructions for my needlepoints are all in chart form. The colours on the charts are not all exact reproductions of the original colours, because they often have to be exaggerated to be distinguishable from the adjacent colours on the chart. The instructions provide the colour numbers.

Before beginning your needlepoint, mark the outer outline of the chart on to the canvas, using a waterproof pen. Allow at least 5cm (2in) extra of unworked canvas outside the outline.

Then trace the outline on to a piece of paper and set this template aside to use later for blocking.

Although it is not absolutely essential, you may find it easier to work from the chart if you mark the grid on to the canvas dividing the threads into tens just like the charted design. Remember that each stitch or square on the chart is equivalent to one canvas intersection and not to a canvas hole.

Blocking

Don't worry if your canvas distorts slightly as your stitching progresses. Wool yarns can be flattened and straightened into shape later by blocking the finished embroidery.

For blocking all you need is a piece of plywood a bit larger than the needlepoint. Lay the completed needlepoint face down and dampen it thoroughly by spraying it with water or using a damp cloth or sponge. Then place the needlepoint face down on the piece of plywood. Using your paper template as your guide, stretch and nail the canvas into shape. Begin with a nail at the centre of each side and then work outwards towards the corners. Let the needlepoint dry completely before removing it, even if it takes several days.

Backing a cushion

Backing a cushion (pillow) is a fairly simple process. Hand or machine stitching are equally suitable.

Begin by cutting the backing fabric, using the blocked and trimmed needlepoint as a guide for size. Cut two pieces of backing fabric, each half the size of the trimmed needlepoint plus an extra seam allowance of 2cm (3/4in) along the centre edge where the zipper will be placed.

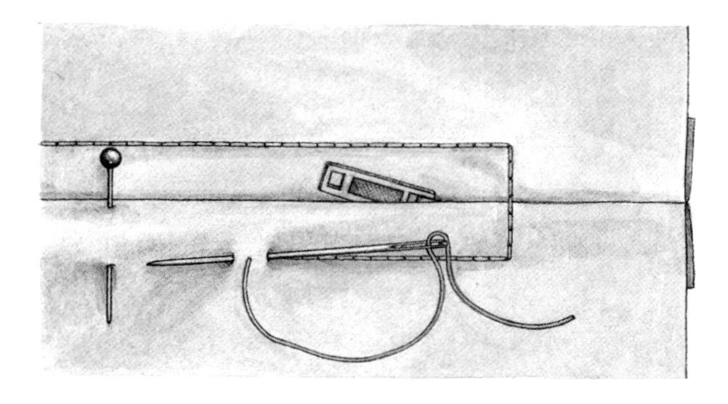

Join the ends of the centre seam, leaving an opening long enough for the zipper. Press open the seam and press back the seam allowance along the zipper opening. Then pin the zipper in place and stitch, using backstitch or a sewing machine with a zipper foot.

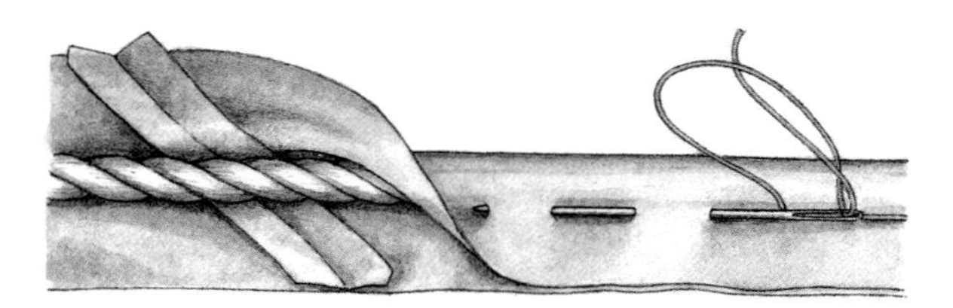

If you are trimming the edge of the cushion (pillow) with piping, you must first cover the cord with bias cut strips of fabric. Fold the fabric strip over the piping (filling) cord and baste close to the cord.

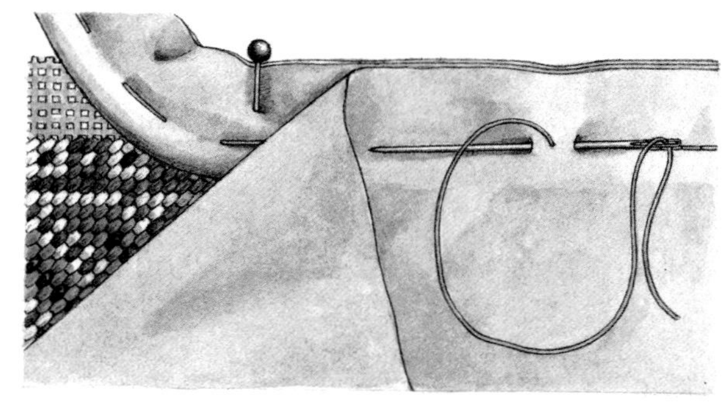

Next pin the covered cord to the right side of the needlepoint lining up the raw edges and the seamlines. Pin the backing over the covered cord so that the right side of the backing and the right side of the needlepoint are facing. Clip the corners of the cushion (pillow) cover and turn right side out.

Collage

Collage is the easiest of all the crafts covered by the projects in this book. After you have gathered together the necessary ingredients, you can achieve quite stunning designs with collage in no time at all. The technique is so simple that it needs little explanation.

Collecting collage

Collage can be made with any type of paper. Arrangements of used stamps are one of my all time favourites for collage (see *Stamps Lampshade* on page 12). Patterned wallpaper can also be cut up and rearranged for effective compositions. More conventional sources for collage are postcards, Sunday newspaper colour supplements and secondhand books.

Collage foundations

Collage can be glued directly on to your wall for an interesting all-over wallpaper (see *Squares Wallpaper Collage* on pages 14 and 15) or for simple borders (see *Pots Border* on page 106). Smaller objects, like lampshades and boxes, are also good vehicles for collage. Free-standing screens are an especially effective foundation because they add a sculptural dimension to the richly patterned surface of collage.

Collage materials

Once you have collected all the necessary paper cutouts and decided on your collage foundation, all you need for making collage is glue and a pair of scissors.

Use wallpaper paste as the adhesive if you are applying a wallpaper collage directly on to the wall. Otherwise use a strong paper glue. Some glues seem at first to make the paper buckle, but the paper then flattens out when the glue is dry. Test your glue on one piece and let it dry completely before using it for the rest of the collage.

Arranging collage pieces

When arranging your collage pieces, try a few juxtapositions of colour before choosing the final one. The best positioning of the cutouts really comes with trial and error. Keep in mind that the collage will appear quite different when whatever surface you are covering is completely covered with detail. Don't loose heart during the process because half-finished work always looks fragmented.

As with any other design that you are improvising as you proceed, you should complete a small area then stand back and study what you have done so far, thinking about what colours to use in the next adjacent area.

After gluing a square foot or so, I flatten the collage with a stack of magazines and reglue any obstinate curling corners. If I am covering a larger area, such as a screen, I begin applying the cutouts at the top and work downwards.

A finished collage may have one or two jarring highlights. After completing my collage, I often glaze over the entire collage with an ochre acrylic wash which will look like old varnish.

Mosaics

Making mosaics is well within the reach of most people. The techniques outlined here are for abstract mosaic designs made with broken ceramics.

Collecting mosaic pieces

To make mosaics you will first of all need a collection of broken ceramics for your mosaic pieces. Save your own chipped, cracked and broken china and put the word out to friends for them to give you theirs.

You might also find bargains at car boot sales. My source of china is flea markets, junk shops, jumble sales and surplus tile shops.

It is easier to store the collected china if it has already broken into pieces. To avoid flying splinters, always put the china in a tough plastic bag before cracking it with a few blows from the hammer. Make sure you have small pieces as well as medium sized ones, as the small pieces are necessary for filling in tiny spaces between the bigger pieces.

Once broken, the ceramic chips are best sorted according to colour and kept in large bowls or flat trays.

Foundations for mosaic

Mosaic can be applied to a wall (in bathrooms for instance) or to any number of household objects.

Some suitable mosaic bases are mirror frames, large vases, ceramic flower pots, metal plates, table tops, and even empty metal movie film cans. Just remember that the foundation must be strong enough to support the combined weight of all the mosaic pieces and grout.

Tools and equipment

Aside from the mosaic base and the china pieces needed to make mosaics, you will also need tile adhesive and tile grout. I use a ready-mixed combined adhesive and grout mixture which can be used for both cementing the pieces in place and for the final grouting of the gaps between the pieces.

The only tool necessary for mosaic making is an artist's small palette knife. This handy tool is ideal for spreading the adhesive, inserting the grout, and scratching excess grout off surface of mosaic pieces. You should also have to hand two soft cloths and a roll of paper towels.

Arranging designs

Most of my own mosaic designs are random, abstract designs built up by forming interesting juxtapositions of colour. Any bold, primitive shape can be attempted in mosaics with satisfying results.

It is a good idea to arrange the mosaic pieces before beginning to fix them in place. This arrangement can be placed directly on the foundation object or on to a paper tracing of the foundation shape. Leave small gaps between the pieces for grouting.

Applying adhesive

Once you have decided on the mosaic arrangement, begin cementing the pieces in place. Read the tile adhesive instructions carefully beforehand. Using the palette knife, spread some adhesive over a small area on the mosaic foundation and push the pieces as close together as possible on the adhesive. Continue in this way working a small area then moving on to the next, until all the mosaic pieces are in place.

Tile adhesive remains soft or malleable for up to an hour, but after that it becomes stiff before setting rock hard. Be careful not to break the adhesive bond by trying to polish at this stage.

Grouting the mosaic

After the adhesive has been left overnight to set, the grout can be applied. Gently scrape off any bits of adhesive on the mosaic pieces before grouting.

The correct grout colour is essential for a successful mosaic design. White grout gives a disappointing effect and makes the mosaic arrangement look dull and bland because it detracts attention from the beauty of the individual china pieces. A darkened grout makes the attractive qualities of the china spring to life. The colour of white grout can be altered by adding grout dye or a touch of acrylic paint before use. If the finished effect is not quite right, you can further darken the set grout with an acrylic wash when the mosaic is finished.

Begin the grouting by inserting it into the gaps with the palette knife. Then using a damp cloth, smear the whole surface of the mosaic with more grout, pushing it into the remaining crevasses. Let the grout set for a short time until it is partially set but not yet hardened. (Twenty minutes of setting will be about right, depending on your tile grout.)

Using a clean damp cloth, wipe the excess grout off the surface of the mosaic. If this is attempted before the grout is slightly set, the cloth will just drag the grout out of the gaps.

Then let the grout set for about another hour and finish the mosaic by polishing each individual piece of china with a paper towel. Any remaining specks of grout on the surface can be scraped off using the palette knife.

Knitting

I'm assuming that you already have basic knitting skills which are, amazingly, all you really need to work the knitted designs in this book. The techniques I cover here are tips for colourwork knitting. I include them as a guide for those knitters who haven't attempted multicoloured knitting and as a reminder for those who haven't picked up their knitting needles for a while.

Multicoloured knitting

People often tend to think that my rich colourwork patterns are difficult to knit, but they are in fact well within the reach of average knitters. Working with a large number of colours seems daunting to many knitters. They fear a never-ending tangle of yarns at the back of the work. I have found that the answer to this problem is a simple one – when working with many colours in one row always use short lengths 60–100cm (2–3ft) long, depending on the size of the area to be covered. As the yarns tangle, it's easy to simply pull through the colour you want to use next. When more of a colour is required you can just start a new short length. So remember to always work with manageable lengths of yarn.

Fair Isle knitting

When two or more colours are used repeatedly across an entire row of knitting, the yarn not being used is carried across the wrong side of the work until it is needed again. This method of colourwork knitting is called 'Fair Isle' knitting.

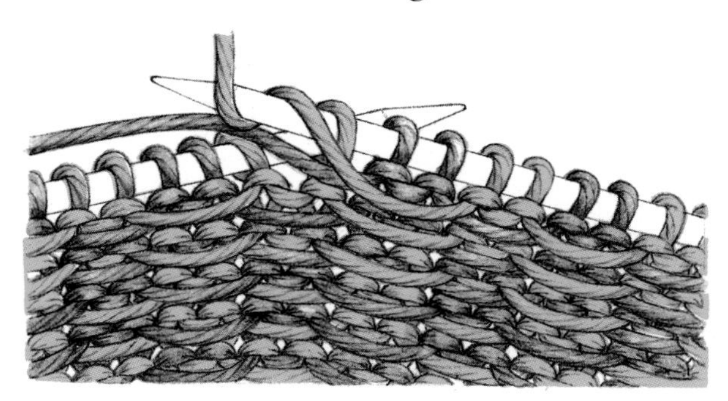

If only a few stitches are spanned by an unused yarn during Fair Isle knitting, it can simply be 'stranded' loosely across (see above).

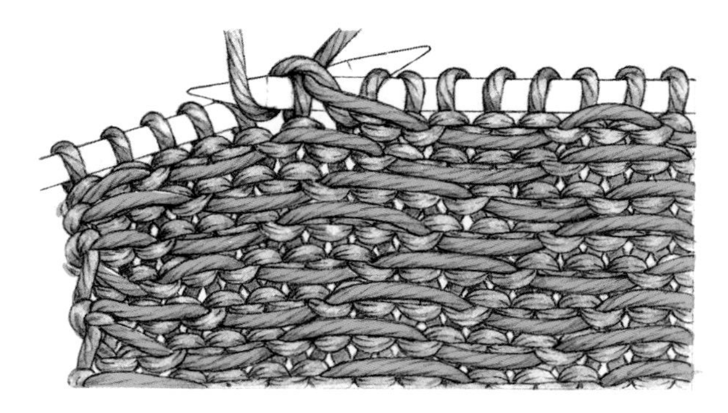

If there are more than about five stitches to span before the yarn is used again, it should be woven under and over the working yarn as you proceed. In this way the loose strand is caught into the back of the knitting. This is called 'weaving-in' or 'knitting-in'. Some knitters like to knit-in on every other stitch, but I find it sufficient to do it on every third stitch or so (see previous page).

Another useful tip I usually give to knitters trying out the Fair Isle technique is to work stranding and weaving-in with a loose and relaxed tension. If you don't, your knitting will pucker and you won't get the smooth surface your are aiming for. It helps to spread out the stitches to their correct width a few times in each row. This keeps the stitches elastic.

Intarsia knitting

The other technique used for multicoloured knitting is called intarsia. This method is used when there are lots of different colours in a row, but each one is only used in a specific area. Instead of carrying a yarn across an entire row, it is simply worked where it is needed and then left hanging at the back until it is needed on the next row.

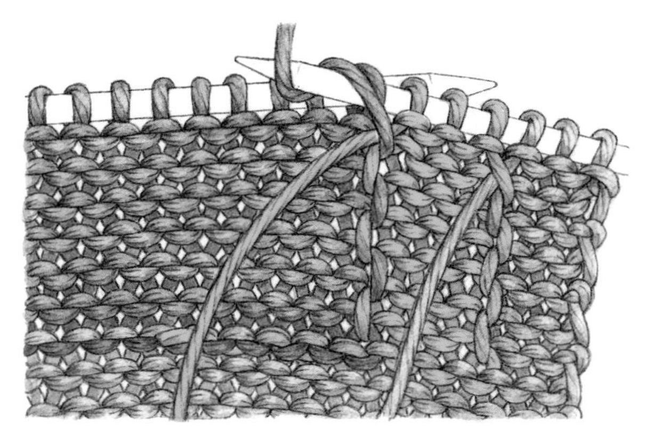

Where the colour change occurs in intarsia knitting, you just twist the two yarns together to avoid holes. In many of my knitting designs, I use both the Fair Isle and intarsia techniques on the same piece of knitting. On the *Leaf Throw* (page 121) for instance, the leaf outline is carried across every row, but the colours for each individual leaf are only used within that leaf.

Knitting-in yarn ends

To save hours of laborious darning-in after a piece of knitting has been completed, I weave in all the yarn ends as I work. The technique for doing this is basically the same as for knitting-in the loose strands or 'floats' in Fair Isle knitting.

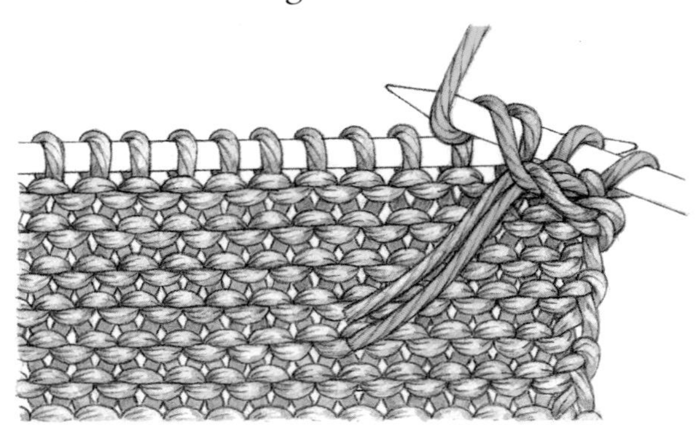

When joining in a new colour, leave 8cm (3in) on both the old and new yarn. Then knit the next two stitches with the new yarn. Holding both ends in your left hand, lay them over the working yarn and work the next stitch.

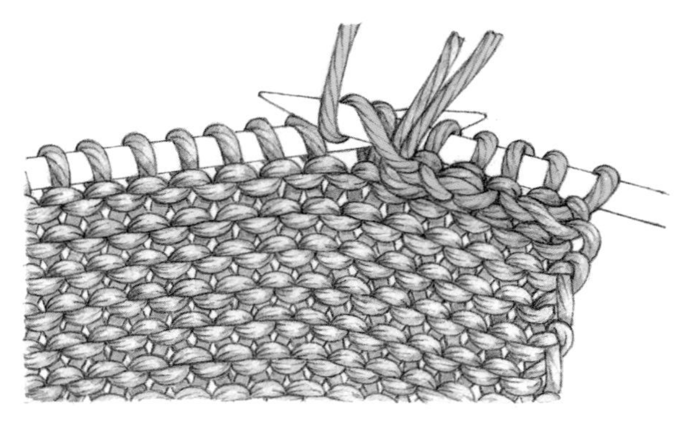

Now insert the right-hand needle in the next stitch in the usual way, bring the ends up behind the working yarn and work the next stitch. Carry on in this way weaving the ends over and under the working yarn until they are completely knitted-in. If you are introducing a new colour but not finishing off the old colour your should weave-in only the end of the new yarn, but in the same way.

Knitting abbreviations

beg	begin(ning)	patt(s)	pattern(s)
cm	centimetre(s)	rem	remain(s)(ing)
cont	continu(e)(ing)	rep	repeat(s)(ing)
dec	decreas(e)(ing)	rnd	round(s)
foll	follow(s)(ing)	RS	right side
g	gram(s)	sl	slip
in	inch(es)	st(s)	stitch(es)
inc	increas(e)(ing)	st st	stocking (stockinette) stitch
k	knit		
m	metre(s)		
mm	millimetre(s)	tog	together
oz	ounce(s)	WS	wrong side
p	purl	yd	yard(s)

* Repeat instructions after asterisk or between asterisks as many times as instructed.

[] Repeat instructions inside brackets as many times as instructed.

Crochet terminology

English-language crochet terminology varies from country to country. There are two distinctly different sets of terminology – those used in Great Britain and those used in the USA. The main difference between the terminology used in Great Britain and the USA is that the basic crochet stitches have different names. The simple crochet instructions given in some of the knitting patterns in this book are written using the British terminology with the US names for the stitches shown in parentheses. The list below gives the name equivalents.

Great Britain		**USA**	
dc	double crochet	sc	single crochet
htr	half treble crochet	hdc	half double crochet
tr	treble crochet	dc	double crochet
dtr	double treble	tr	triple
trtr	triple treble	dtr	double treble
qtr	quadruple treble	trtr	triple treble

Yarns and Kits

Needlepoint Yarns

The following needlepoint yarns have been used for the needlepoint designs in this book. The lengths given by yarn manufacturers for skeins and hanks are approximate. Although the instructions call for a specific number of small skeins, you can purchase larger skeins/hanks if a large amount of the colour is required and if a larger skein/hank is available.

APPLETON *Tapestry Wool*
10m (11yd) per skein
55m (60yd) per hank
PATERNA/YAN *Persian Yarn*
three 7.4m (8yd) strands per small skein
three 36m (40yd) strands per large skein
three 155m (170yd) strands per hank
ANCHOR *Tapisserie Wool*
10m (11yd) per skein

Appleton *Tapestry Wool* and Anchor *Tapisserie Wool* are all 100 per cent wool 'tapestry weight' needlepoint yarns and one strand is sufficient for working on a 10-mesh canvas.

Paterna (Paternayan) *Persian Yarn* is a finer wool yarn that comes in a length of three separable strands. Two or three strands of *Persian Yarn* are sufficient for working tent stitch on a 10-mesh canvas. Even when all three strands of *Persian Yarn* are used together, the yarn will lie more smoothly on the canvas if the strands are separated and put back together before use.

Yarn amounts

The yarn amounts given in the needlepoint instructions in this book are generous and will be sufficient for an embroidery worked entirely in continental (or basketweave) tent stitch. If you use the half cross stitch technique (see page 151) throughout, instead of the continental (or basketweave) tent stitch technique, you may find that you use as much as 20 to 30 per cent less than the specified amounts.

Needlepoint kits from Ehrman

The Kaffe Fassett designs which are featured in this book and are available as kits from Ehrman are as follows:

Ordering needlepoint kits

To order Kaffe Fassett needlepoint kits contact one of the following addresses:

UK: EHRMAN (shop), 14-16 Lancer Square, Kensington Church Street, London W8 4EP, England. Tel: (0171) 937 8123.
USA: EHRMAN, 5 Northern Boulevard, Amherst, New Hampshire 03031. Tel: (800) 433 7899.
Canada: POINTERS, 1017 Mount Pleasant Road, Toronto, Ontario M4P 2MI. Tel: (416) 322 9461.
Australia: TAPESTRY ROSE, PO Box 366, Canterbury 3126. Tel: (3) 818 6022.
New Zealand: QUALITY HANDCRAFTS, PO Box 1486, Auckland. Tel: (09) 411 8645.
Argentina: VICKIMPORT SA, 25 de Mayo 596, Sp (1002) Buenos Aires. Tel: 322 4247.
Belgium and Holland: HEDERA, Diestsestraat 172, 3000 Leuven. Tel: 016 235997.
Denmark: DESIGNER GARN, Vesterbro 33A, DK 9000 Aalborg. Tel: 9813 4824.
Finland: NOVITA, PO Box 59, 00211 Helsinki. Tel: 358 067 3176.
France: ARMADA, Collange, Lournand, Cluny 71250. Tel: 85 59 1356.
Germany: OFFERTA VERSAND, Bruneckerstrasse 2a, D–6080 Gross-Gerau. Tel: 06152 56964.
Iceland: STORKURINN, Kjorgardi, Laugavegi 159, 101 Reykjavik. Tel: 01 18258.
Italy: SYBILLA, D & C Spa Divisione Sybilla, Via Nannetti, 40069 Zola Predosa. Tel: 051 750 875.
Spain: CANVAS AND TAPESTRY, Costanila de los Angelez, 28013 Madrid.
Sweden: WINCENT, Svearvagen 94, 113 50 Stockholm. Tel: 8673 7060.
Switzerland: BOPP INTERIEUR AG, Poststrasse 1, CH–8001 Zurich. Tel: 1 211 6203.

Needlepoint yarn suppliers

The needlepoint yarns used in this book are widely available in specialist needlework shops and in large department stores. To find a stockist near you, see the following;

or contact the yarn companies or the distributors listed here.

Appleton yarns main office in UK
APPLETON BROS LTD, Thames Works, Church Street, Chiswick, London W4 2PE, England. Tel: (0181) 994 0711. Fax: (0181) 995 6609.

Appleton mail order in USA
Rose Cottage stock the full range of Appleton yarns and provides a mail order service:
ROSE COTTAGE, 209 Richmond Street, El Segundo, California 90245.
Tel: (310) 322 8225. Fax: (310) 322 0187.

Appleton stockists in USA
Appleton yarn is available in many retail outlets throughout the USA. The following are a few selected US stockists and distributors:

Alabama
PATCHES & STITCHES, 817A Regal Drive, Huntsville, Alabama 35801.
Tel: (205) 533 3897.
SALLY S. BOOM, Wildwood Studio, PO Box 303, Montrose, Alabama 36559.
Village Needlecraft Inc, 7500 South Memorial Pkwy, Unit 116, Huntsville, Alabama 35802.

California
FLEUR DE PARIS, 5835 Washington Boulevard, Culver City, California 90230.
Tel: (800) 221 6453.
HANDCRAFT FROM EUROPE, PO Box 31524, San Francisco, California 94131-0524.
NATALIE, 144 North Larchmont Boulevard, Los Angeles, California 90004.
NEEDLEPOINT INC, 251 Post Street, 2nd Floor, San Francisco, California 94108.
Tel: (415) 392 1622.
ROSE COTTAGE, 209 Richmond Street, El Segundo, California 90245.
Tel: (310) 322 8225. Fax: (310) 322 0187.
(See *mail order* above.)

Delaware
THE JOLLY NEEDLEWOMAN, 5810 Kennett Pike, Centreville, Delaware 19807.
Tel: (302) 658 9585.

Louisiana
NEEDLE ARTS STUDIO, 115 Metairie Road, Metairie, Louisiana 70005.
Tel: (504) 832 3050.

Maryland
THE ELEGANT NEEDLE LTD, 7945 MacArthur Boulevard, Suite 203, Cabin John, Maryland 20818.

Massachusetts
STITCHES OF THE PAST, 68 Park Street, Andover, Massachusetts 01810.
Tel: (508) 683 3146.

Missouri
SIGN OF THE ARROW, 1867 Foundation Inc, 9740 Clayton Road, St Louis, Missouri 63124. Tel: (314) 994 0606.

Ohio
LOUISE'S NEEDLEWORK, 45 North High Street, Dublin, Ohio 43017.
Tel: (614) 792 3505.

Pennsylvania
EWE TWO LTD, 24 North Merion Avenue, Bryn Mawr, Pennsylvania 19010.
Tel: (215) 527 3306.

Wisconsin
PRINCESS AND THE PEA, 1922 Parminter Street, Middleton, Wisconsin 53562.

Texas
ACCESS COMMODITIES (L. Haidar), PO Box 1778, Rockwall, Texas 75087.
Tel: (214) 722 1211. Fax: (214) 722 1302.
CHAPARRAL, 3701 West Alabama, Suite 370, Houston, Texas 77027.
Tel: (713) 621 7562.
DAN'S FIFTH AVENUE, 1520 Fifth Avenue, Canyon, Texas 79015.

Appleton stockists in Canada
DICK AND JANE, 2352 West 41st Avenue, Vancouver, British Columbia V6M 2A4.
Tel: (604) 738 3574.
FANCYWORKS, 104-3960 Quera Street, Victoria, British Columbia V8X 4A3.
Tel: (604) 727 2765.
JET HANDCRAFT STUDIO LTD, PO Box 91103, 225 17th Street, West Vancouver, British Columbia V7V 3N3.
ONE STITCH AT A TIME, PO Box 114, Picton, Ontario K0K 2T0.

Appleton stockists in Australia
CLIFTON H JOSEPH & SON (AUSTRALIA) PTY LTD, 391-393 Little Lonsdale Street, Melbourne, Victoria 3000.
Tel: (03) 602 1222.
STADIA HANDCRAFTS, 85 Elizabeth Street, Paddington, New South Wales 2021.
Tel: (02) 328 7973.
P L STONEWALL & CO PTY LTD (Flag Division), 52 Erskine Street, Sydney.

Appleton stockists in New Zealand
NANCY'S EMBROIDERY LTD, 326 Tinakori Road, PO Box 245, Thorndon, Wellington. Tel: (04) 473 4047.

Anchor yarns
UK: COATS PATONS CRAFTS, McMullen Road, Darlington, County Durham DL1 1YQ, England. Tel: (01325) 36 54 57. Fax: (01325) 38 23 00.
USA: COATS AND CLARK, Susan Bates Inc, 30 Patewood Drive, Greenville, South Carolina 29615. Tel: 1 800 241 5997.
Canada: COATS PATONS CANADA, 1001 Roselawn Avenue, Toronto, Ontario M6B 1B8. Tel: (416) 782 4481. Toll free: 1 800 268 3620. Fax: (416) 785 1370.
Australia: COATS PATONS CRAFTS, 89-91 Peters Avenue, Mulgrave, Victoria 3170. Tel: (03) 561 2288. Fax: (03) 561 2298.
New Zealand: COATS ENZED CRAFTS, East Tamaki, Auckland. Tel: (09) 274 0116. Fax: (09) 274 0584.

Paterna/Paternayan yarns
UK: PATERNA LTD, PO Box 1, Ossett, West Yorkshire WF5 9SA, England. Tel: (01924) 81 19 04. Fax: (01924) 81 08 18.
USA: Paternayan, JCA Inc, 35 Scales Lane, Townsend, Massachusetts 01469.
Tel: (508) 597 8794.
Australia: STADIA HANDCRAFTS, 85 Elizabeth Street (PO Box 495), Paddington, New South Wales 2021.
Tel: (02) 328 7973. Fax: (02) 326 1768.
Canada: See USA.
New Zealand: THE STITCHING CO LTD, PO 74-269 Market Road, Auckland.
Tel: (09) 366 6080. Fax: (09) 366 6040.

Knitting Yarns

It is always best to use the yarn recommended in the knitting pattern instructions. Addresses for the suppliers of the knitting yarns used in this book are listed opposite.

If you want to use a substitute yarn, choose a yarn of the same type and weight as the recommended yarn. The descriptions (below) of the various yarns are meant as a guide to the yarn weight. Remember that the description of the yarn weight is only a rough guide and you should test a yarn first to see if it will achieve the correct stitch gauge.

The amount of a substitute yarn needed is determined by the number of metres (yards) required rather than by the number of grams (ounces). If you are unsure when choosing a suitable substitute, ask your yarn shop to assist you.

Knitting yarn descriptions

PATERNA/YAN *Persian Yarn* – the three strands of this embroidery yarn used together are roughly equivalent to an Aran weight knitting yarn
100% wool
three 7.4m (8yd) strands per small skein
three 36m (40yd) strands per large skein
three 155m (170yd) strands per hank

ROWAN *Donegal Lambswool Tweed* – a 4-ply (US sport) weight knitting yarn
100% pure new wool
approx 100m (109yd) per 25g (1oz) hank

ROWAN *Kid Silk* – a 4-ply (US sport) weight knitting yarn

70% kid mohair and 30% mulberry silk
approx 62m (67yd) per 25g (1oz) hank

ROWAN *Lightweight DK* – a lightweight double knitting (US sport) weight yarn
100% pure new wool
approx 67m (73yd) per 25g (1oz) hank

Paterna/Paternayan yarns
Paterna/Paternayan *Persian Yarn* is a needlepoint yarn and the suppliers' addresses are listed under *Needlepoint Yarns*.

When purchasing Persian Yarn for knitting, be sure to purchase continuous skeins/hanks instead of lengths already precut for needlepoint.

Rowan yarns
UK: ROWAN, Green Lane Mill, Holmfirth, West Yorkshire HD7 1RW, England. Tel: (0484) 68 18 81. Fax: (0484) 68 79 20.
USA: WESTMINSTER TRADING CORPORATION, 5 Northern Boulevard, Amherst, New Hampshire 03031. Tel: (603) 886 5041/5043.
Australia: ROWAN (AUSTRALIA), 191 Canterbury Road, Canterbury, Victoria 3126. Tel: (03) 830 1609.
Belgium: HEDERA, Pleinstraat 68, 3001 Leuven. Tel: (016) 23 21 89.
Canada: ESTELLE DESIGNS & SALES LTD, Units 65/67, 2220 Midland Avenue, Scarborough, Ontario M1P 3E6. Tel: (416) 298 9922.
Denmark: DESIGNER GARN, Vesterbro 33 A, DK–9000 Aalborg. Tel: 98 13 48 24.
France: Sidel, Chemin Departemental 14C, 13840 Rognes. Tel: (33) 42 50 15 06.
Germany: WOLLE AND DESIGN, Wolfshovener Strasse 76, 52428 Julich-Stetternich. Tel: 02461/54735.
Holland: HENK & HENRIETTA BEUKERS, Dorpsstraat 9, NL5327 AR Hurwenen. Tel: 04182 1764.
Iceland: STORKURINN, Kjorgardi, Laugavegi 59, ICE–101 Reykjavik. Tel: (01) 18258.
Italy: LA COMPAGNIA DEL COTONE, Via Mazzini 44, I–10123, Torino. Tel: (011) 87 83 81.
Japan: DIAKEITO CO LTD, 2–3–11 Senba-Higashi, Minoh City, Osaka 562. Tel: 0727 27 6604.
New Zealand: JOHN Q GOLDINGHAM Ltd, PO Box 45083, Epuni Railway, Lower Hutt. Tel: (04) 5674 085 or (04) 5674 094.
Norway: EUREKA, PO Box 357, N–1401 Ski. Tel: 64 86 55 40.
Sweden: WINCENT, Sveavagen 94, 113 50 Stockholm. Tel: (08) 673 70 60.

Props Credits

pages **34–35** Curtain fabric by Kaffe Fassett from Brunschwig & Fils. *pages* **56–57** Masks from Kalimantan Creations, The Livery Stables Market, Chalk Farm Road, London NW1 BAH. *pages* **74–75** Curtain fabric by Kaffe Fassett from Designers Guild, 277 Kings Road, London SW3 5EN. *page* **84** Wallpaper border by Kaffe Fassett from Designers Guild (address as before). *pages* **90–91** Chairs from Mollie Evans, 82 Hill Rise, Richmond, Surrey TW10 6UB; and fabric wallcovering by Kaffe Fassett from Designers Guild (address as before). *page* **104** Green shelves from Kalimantan Creations; and wallpaper by Kaffe Fassett from Designers Guild (addresses as before). *pages* **110–111** Majolica ware from Britannia, 58 Davies Street, London W1; wallpaper from Alexander Beauchamp, Vulcan House, Stratton Road, Gloucester GL1 4HL; woven tapestry from Belinda Coote Tapestries, 29 Holland Street, London W8 4NA; and *B*egonia needlepoint hanging by designer Jill Gordon (available as a kit from Ehrman). *pages* **132–133** Wallpaper from Sanderson. *page* **141** Wallpaper from Alexander Beauchamp (address as before).

Photo Credits

The publishers would like to thank the following for permission to use illustrations:

AKG London /Erich Lessing *93 top*; Ancient Art and Architecture Collection / Elly Beintema *38 bottom*; Angelo Hornak Library *113*; Peter Aprahamian *140 right*; Arcaid /Richard Bryant *77 top*; Arcaid / Lucinda Lambton *16 top right*; Artephot / Nimatallah *67 top*; Bridgeman Art Library /Bonhams *52*; Bridgeman Art Library *112 bottom*; Christie's Images *16 top left*; Edifice /Darley *8, 84*; The Interior World /Schulenburg *112 top*; The Interior World /Francesco Venturi *92*; Koninklijk Museum (Yoor Schone Kunsten), Antwerp /© DACS 1995 *58 right*; Miya Kosei *10 right, 102 top, 134 top*; National Trust Photographic Library /Andreas von Einsiedel *66 bottom*; Photothèque des Musées de la Ville de Paris /© DACS 1995 *135*; Robert Harding Picture Library *77 bottom*; Royal Geographical Society /Jim Holmes *10 left, 60 bottom*; TLC Designs, New York *48 top*; Weidenfeld and Nicolson /Victoria and Albert Museum *93 bottom*; Jeremy Whitaker MCSD *38 top*.

Acknowledgements

The older I get the more I love working in a team. After spending my early years as a lonely painter, I now find it a great luxury to have the stimulation of like-minded input. A book like this, with such intensely detailed sets, needs a lot of co-operation.

Firstly, thanks for all the stitching of needlepoint, and knitting of cushions and throws to Maria, Jules, David, Charlotte, Eleanor, Belinda and Yvonne. Grateful thanks also to the volunteer students Traji, Sophie, Sarah, Karen, Nicci and Adele.

For the dedicated hours of work on the editing, layout and the book planning – warm thanks to the team of Sally Harding, Polly Dawes and Denise Bates.

For the set construction, painting and paper hanging – thanks to Sue Black, Jonathan Brown and Yair Meshoulam.

Grateful thanks indeed go to my suppliers of gorgeous props and papers: Brunschwig & Fils for shell fabric, Belinda Coote for the woven tapestry, Kalimantan for the masks and the carved pot stands, Rita Smyth of Britannia for the majolica tableware, Alexander Beauchamp for the stunning wallpaper murals and Sandersons' for the flowery wallpapers. A special thanks to Tricia Guild for encouraging me to design fabrics and wallpapers and letting me use them so extravagantly.

It is always a thrill to meet fellow enthusiasts who encourage me on my path of obsession. I would like to pay tribute to two such enthusiasts – Sue Godley whose house is a perfect living example of my designer dreams, and Christian Lacroix whose book *Pieces of a Pattern* was a gigantic inspiration as I started this book.

Lastly, thanks in abundance to two people without whom this book could never have existed – to my assistant Brandon Mably who oversaw every aspect of the project and choreographed all our meetings, and to Debbie Patterson whose unfailing good humour, creative ideas and stunning photography never cease to amaze us all!

Index

Page numbers in *italic* refer to illustrations. Designs in **bold** have instructions.